Campfires
and Loon Calls
Travels in the Boundary Waters

Jerry Apps
Photographs by Steve Apps

FULCRUM
GOLDEN, COLORADO

Library of Congress Cataloging-in-Publication Data
Apps, Jerold W., 1934-
  Campfires and loon calls : travels in the Boundary Waters / Jerry Apps
; photography by Steve Apps.
      p. cm.
  Includes bibliographical references.
  ISBN 978-1-936218-07-3 (pbk.)
  1. Canoe camping--Minnesota--Boundary Waters Canoe Area. 2.
Canoes
and canoeing--Minnesota--Boundary Waters Canoe Area. 3. Outdoor
recreation--Minnesota--Boundary Waters Canoe Area. 4. Wilderness
areas--Minnesota--Boundary Waters Canoe Area. 5. Boundary Waters
Canoe
Area (Minn.)--Guidebooks. I. Apps, Steve. II. Title.
  GV790.A67 2011
  796.5409776'75--dc22
                              2010045853

Printed in the United States of America
0 9 8 7 6 5 4 3 2 1

Design: Jack Lenzo
Cover image © Steve Apps

Fulcrum Publishing
4690 Table Mountain Drive, Suite 100
Golden, Colorado 80403
800-992-2908 • 303-277-1623
www.fulcrumbooks.com

Dedicated to
the thousands of canoeists
who have looked for and found peace
in the Boundary Waters Canoe Area Wilderness

Contents

Acknowledgments

Many people made this book possible, some without being aware of their contributions. My father, who died in 1993, instilled in me a love for the outdoors, a curiosity to learn more about it, and the patience to become a part of it. My friend and colleague Walter Bjoraker introduced me to canoes and canoeing more than forty years ago, and canoes have intrigued me ever since. My son Steve first introduced me to the Boundary Waters Canoe Area Wilderness in 1983. I was awed at the place then. I still am.

Several people helped in the preparation of this book. My never-tiring wife, Ruth, reads all my manuscripts, this one included, and offers many suggestions for improvement. My son Jeff, a banker in Colorado and my canoe companion on several trips, made important suggestions for improving the book. My daughter, Susan, also read segments and made improvements. Kate Thompson was also exceedingly helpful in fine-tuning this book. I want to especially thank Sam Scinta of Fulcrum Publishing for his interest in this project and his support throughout the development of the book. Many others contributed. I thank each of them.

A tent, a canoe, a campfire, and a lake view all make for enjoyable wilderness camping.

Introduction

I went to the woods because I wished to live deliberately,
to front only the essential facts of life,
and see if I could not learn what it had to teach,
and not, when I came to die, discover that I had not lived.

—Henry David Thoreau, *Walden*

I've learned much from twenty-five years of canoe camping in the Boundary Waters. And I have a lot more to learn. What I'm most noted for is missing portages and getting lost. (Ask my canoeing companions about this, especially my children, Sue, Steve, and Jeff, who have been with me when I've been hopelessly misplaced with no hint of how to get back to our campsite. Of course, some of our most interesting experiences have occurred when we were lost.) On these pages, I share some of what I've learned with the hope that others might find the information helpful—or in some cases, learn from my example what *not* to do.

I must confess that what I have gained from twenty-five years of smoky campfires and eerie loon calls in the night goes well beyond paddling and camping skills. This place with the long set of initials has helped me tap into something more profound than skill learning, even more important than how to survive a wicked thunderstorm. The BWCAW has reminded me that I am just one little piece in this complicated and often mysterious puzzle of nature. It is an awesome consideration. I've learned to slow down and take things as they come, to enjoy an experience that is often different from what I had intended, or even hoped for.

Thoreau wrote, "Most of the luxuries, and many of the so-called comforts of life, are not only not indispensable, but positive hindrances to the elevation of mankind."[1] These words describe one of my reasons for returning to the Boundary Waters each year, as I leave behind the luxuries and comforts of my life and appreciate once more the power of simplicity. I step away from a life that's complicated by electronic gadgetry to master, elaborate schedules to meet, performance outcomes to consider, and a rush, rush, rush perspective. In the Boundary Waters, all of that is on hold and unplugged. I'm back to a life that I knew as a child, when we had no electricity, my mother cooked on a wood-burning stove, and we walked a mile to our country school. I'm continually reminded to listen, smell, taste, feel, and see—autumn's first yellow leaf, a giant bull moose eating pond plants, the subtle sound of thunder in the distance, the feel of a rocky portage underfoot, the smell of clean air, the taste of fresh-caught fish for supper. All my senses are in play.

As I researched and wrote this book, I was struck by the long and tortuous struggle to establish and protect the Boundary Waters Canoe Area Wilderness from development. The struggle continues today—in the Boundary Waters and throughout the country—as wilderness areas and other environmentally sensitive places are constantly attacked and eroded. The debate often comes down to a fundamental question: What good is a wilderness area? What is its *value*? On my farm in central Wisconsin I have a substantial population of Karner blue butterflies, a federally endangered species that relies on the lupines that grow in profusion here. An acquaintance once asked me, what good are those butterflies? What's their value? Why do you spend time encouraging lupines to grow on your farm when you could grow a more profitable crop? Of course, the word lurking behind these questions is *money*. For some people, something's value depends solely on whether or not it can bring a monetary return. In the case of my little butterflies, encouraging them *just because they are there* seems a weak defense to these folks.

Some of the most important values have little to do with money, luxury, or the accumulation of things: patience, silence, solitude, simplicity, and contemplation. Experiencing a wilderness area like the BWCAW can help people reclaim some of these lost values and help them rediscover—or discover for the first time—what it means to be human. Once you have spent time where clocks and watches are irrelevant, where the only sounds are those of the loon, the wind in the trees, and waves slapping against shore rocks, your perspective changes. And when you know a place that affects you profoundly, the more likely you are to revere and protect it. The more people know a place like the BWCAW and its stories, the more likely they will be alert to environmental challenges, such as land-use decisions, climate-change policy, attitudes toward endangered species, developing future energy sources, and so on.

Knowing happens at several levels, starting with learning the facts of a place's history, geography, geology, and ecology, and then moving to the stories about the place. Stories give a place an identity and a deeper meaning. In my Boundary Waters journals I keep a record of all my trips. I referred to these journals and the stories recorded there often while writing this book. The stories take me where my emotions, beliefs, and values reside. Stories help me know a place—and in turn know a little bit more about myself.

The need to connect with nature is in our genetic makeup, for whether we accept it or not, we are a part of nature. When we arrogantly try to subdue nature, we are in effect subduing ourselves, making ourselves less whole. And when we deliberately or accidentally destroy a part of nature—failing to protect an endangered species, allowing land to be misused, polluting a waterway—we destroy a little of ourselves. When we accept that we are a part of nature, we take an important step toward appreciating, understanding, and protecting the environment.

Richard Louv, in his book *Last Child in the Woods,* eloquently reminds us to encourage our children to experience nature and the joys associated with wilderness. Louv writes, "Nature inspires creativity in a child by demanding visualization and full use of the senses. Given a chance, a child will bring the confusion of the world to the woods, wash it in the creek, turn it over to see what lives on the unseen side of that confusion."[2] Too often these days, parents feel compelled to protect their children from the "dangers" associated with nature—insect bites, sunburn, challenging weather. As a result, children often become mere spectators rather than participants in nature. They watch videos, search the Web, and participate in virtual nature activities. But the difference between virtual and the real thing is as profound as the difference between sitting by a real campfire and watching a virtual campfire on a TV screen. Experiencing the smells, tastes, sounds, sights, and feelings of the outdoors makes all the difference. Ultimately, it is these future generations who will make decisions about the need for wilderness and the obligation to live a lifestyle that protects the environment. It is our responsibility to help them see, as Thoreau did, that "in wilderness is the preservation of the world."

Throughout this book, I share what the Boundary Waters Canoe Area Wilderness has meant to me, but much of the deeper meaning is difficult to put into words. There is something about experiencing wilderness that goes to the depths of a person's humanity and reaches a place untouched in many people's lives. A wilderness experience touches our souls.

*Wilderness canoe camping is a time for relaxation and rejuvenation,
a time to once more experience simplicity and reconnect with nature.*

Part I: Beginnings

Beauty is composed of many things and never stands alone.
It is part of the horizons, blue in the distance,
great primeval silences, knowledge of all things of the earth.

—Sigurd Olson, *Reflections from the North Country*

First Trip

I unfold our map and find Round Lake. We are three lakes and two portages away from entering the Boundary Waters Canoe Area Wilderness. We begin loading the gear into our 17-foot aluminum Grumman canoe.

"Do we need this much stuff?" Steve asks as we pile the canoe high.

"You agreed to it all," I say.

"Next year we'll do better," he says after pushing the last bag into an unused corner of the canoe. By doing better I'm sure he means bringing a lot less gear—or at least lighter gear.

Soon we are paddling. The morning has turned clear and warm with little wind, so the paddling is easy. Before long, we've gotten into a rhythm that sends the loaded canoe easily through the water, its bow making little gurgling sounds. Steve paddles and steers from the back and I paddle in the front, our gear piled between us. Neither of us says anything as we move silently through the water. I paddle as quietly as I can, thrust, pull, thrust, pull, moving us along but not wanting to interfere with the silence.

Round Lake is about 155 acres and 45 feet deep. After about a mile of paddling, we reach the portage leading to West Round Lake and unload the canoe. With Steve's tutelage, I learn the trick for tipping the canoe over and lifting it on its end so he can slip under and balance the craft on his shoulders. He pulls on one of the packs, I help him hoist the canoe onto his back, and he is off. At this point I cross my fingers that our makeshift yoke, held in place with duct tape, will remain in place. It does.

At the end of the portage, we load everything back into the canoe and make the short paddle across West Round Lake in search of the 50-rod (a rod is 5.5 yards, or 16.5 feet) portage to Edith Lake. According to the map, the boundary line for the BWCAW cuts across the west end of Edith Lake and intersects the portage to Brant Lake, which appears fully within the BWCAW. We paddle across little Edith Lake to the 36-rod portage to Brant Lake. The portages so far have been reasonable—relatively flat but a bit muddy. Steve slogs along the trail with the canoe and a pack, not complaining. I carry a single pack and begin working up a sweat. This is supposed to be fun. Sweating for me usually means work. In the low, marshy places along the portage route mosquitoes find us, swarms of them that attack us without mercy. Steve hates them more than I do, because while carrying the canoe he can't swat them as they drill into his neck and back. Until this point we have seen no mosquitoes, so we haven't put on any repellant. We suffer because of our delinquency.

It is a pleasant paddle in Brant Lake in search of the portage to Gotter Lake, a rather small lake with several islands. We find the portage with little difficulty—surprise, surprise. By this time I've decided that the people who establish portages take great delight in making the portage entrances well-nigh impossible to find. I suspect this is supposed to be some of the fun of canoeing, searching for a portage and trying to decide how accurate the maps are in declaring their location. Maybe it's just me, but a hidden portage entrance quickly becomes an annoyance. And how am I supposed to know the difference between a portage and a game trail where a moose has come to the lake for a drink? I know, I'm supposed to be relaxed and laid-back when I'm canoeing. Mostly I am. But not being able to find a portage ranks right up there with swarms of mosquitoes and menacing black flies.

A quick paddle across Gotter Lake followed by a 50-rod portage and we are in long and narrow Flying Lake, which we follow to Flying Creek. Then a 15-rod portage to a short, interesting paddle in Bingshick Creek, another 13-rod portage, and we reach our goal for the day, Bingshick Lake. I am bushed. My shoulders ache, my back hurts. I have too many mosquito bites. So far we have paddled in seven lakes and portaged 341 rods (1,875.5 yards, or a little over a mile) all on our first day. BWCAW portages are not a walk in the park on well-groomed, sawdust-covered trails. They are hilly, rocky, sometimes wet and muddy, often slippery, and occasionally blocked by a tree that has decided to fall inconveniently across the path. Of course we tote heavy packs, and Steve also carries a canoe. But canoeists are a strange lot, by and large. Seldom do you hear anyone complaining about portages. They are part of the experience and soon become the stuff of canoe stories that tend to be embellished over the years. Nonetheless, portages are hard work, especially for those of us who spend too much time indoors and seldom lift more than a pencil during the day's activity.

We search for a campsite on Bingshick Lake. Campsites are blessedly easier to locate than portages, mostly because you can spot where people have pulled up the canoes and trampled down the grass. Of course, spotting the ever-present fire grate is the final confirmation that you indeed have found a Forest Service–designated campsite, an approved, legal place to camp. According to our map, Bingshick has but two campsites, both on the north side of the lake. I also note that the Kekekabic Hiking Trail cuts by the north side of the lake, so I anticipate seeing a hiker or two plodding along the trail.

Bingshick is about 44 acres, only three-quarters of a mile long and about one-eighth of a mile wide, but we quickly see that it's a beautiful little lake. We pull in at the easternmost campsite and set up camp.

Later I make my first journal entry for the trip:

Tuesday, August 16, 1983. Bingshick Lake
We arrived at the campsite on Bingshick about 1:00 PM. As we began setting up our camp, four loons flew over, calling. The first loon call I had ever heard, and I stopped to watch and listen. The loon call is amazing. Nothing like it. Mysterious. Eerie. Prehistoric. Earlier this morning, we saw several ducks and a bull moose when we drove to our launch site.

We pitched our tent on a rocky site that juts out into the lake. The site is high enough so a breeze seems to always blow, driving away any mosquitoes lurking in the area as well as discouraging any menacing deerflies left over from early summer. Our tent is a considerably used, orange, four-person Eureka that we borrowed from a neighbor.

About 3:00 PM it began raining lightly, and it still is. I am writing this sitting under a big white pine tree, so far so good, I'm staying dry. Steve is reading in the tent. It's a relaxing afternoon.

By suppertime the rain stops. I fire up my new camp stove, boil some water, make two cups of instant vegetable soup (more like petrified vegetables lost in too much salt; surprising how hunger can improve the quality of food), and soon have our first meal of macaroni and cheese ready to eat. I am declared camp cook.

"Whoever owns the stove is the cook," says Steve. I believe he remembers that I am a terrible cook, right up there with my father, who couldn't boil water without burning it. No complaints about the macaroni and cheese, though. The camp cook is off to a good start. We sit on logs that surround the fire grate, eating and watching a pair of loons cruising a few yards in front of the campsite and serenading us with dinner music. Chocolate pudding for dessert. I boil another pot of water, and we sit enjoying instant coffee, the loons, and the smells of the outdoors. After so much time spent in the city, one tends to forget the smell of pine needles, the subtle smell of lake water, and the dense, musky smell of humid night air.

And the sounds—the quiet sounds of water gently lapping against the rocks, the scurrying of a red

This was our campsite in 1983.

squirrel visiting the campsite in search of a dropped crumb, the rustling of pine needles as a slight, cooling breeze blows in from the lake. The loons are quiet now.

I listen for the most profound sound of all, the sound of silence. There's none of the background traffic noise that is ever-present in cities and most rural areas, no man-made sounds at all here in this wilderness area.

I am thrust back to my growing-up years on a farm during the latter years of the Great Depression, when my dad, mother, brothers, and I sat on the back porch of the old farmhouse in early evening after the chores were done. Pa instructed us to listen for the sounds of the night, but on many quiet summer evenings there was no sound, save perhaps for the distant *dong, dong* of a cowbell in a neighbor's pasture half a mile away.

I remember walking with Dad in the woods on a summer day. "Walk quietly," he'd say. "And no talking." He wanted me to tune in to my surroundings, the sounds and sights of the out-of-doors. Now, as I sit looking out over the quiet waters of Bingshick Lake, I am back to my childhood and the lessons I learned from my father about paying attention to my surroundings—the sights and sounds and feelings. Tonight I will sleep well, embraced by the sounds of the night.

❧

It is warm when I awaken this morning. Dew hangs heavy on everything, dripping from the trees and wetting the tent's rain fly. I feel the previous day's

Wilderness camping is a good time for reading, or for just doing nothing and feeling good about it.

activities; my shoulders ache from portaging the heavy packs and my arms hurt from paddling. I will share none of this with Steve, who is sleeping in. A father doesn't want his son to know he is an out-of-shape wimp. I pour some white gas into the camp stove, pump it up with the built-in pump, light it, and soon I have water boiling. I lower the food bag from its place high in a tree and away from bears and other critters intent on sharing our meals, and I find the bag marked Breakfast. I make myself a cup of instant coffee and spend the next half hour doing nothing except looking out over the quiet waters of

Bingshick Lake, watching wisps of fog rise from the cool water. It has been a long time since I spent time doing nothing. It's a good feeling. A liberating feeling. I give myself permission to just sit. But of course I feel I need a reason for this nonproductive behavior. The loud voice in my head that keeps driving me forward is yelling, "Those who just sit are lazy and not worth much!" I need a response to the voice's concerns. *Recuperating* is my answer. I am weary and sore from the previous day's work. But a quieter voice, one deep in the back of my mind, is whispering, "You need some do-nothing time. Doing nothing from time to time is okay."

With Steve up—moving, smiling, and not complaining at all about a sore back, shoulders, or anything else—I begin cooking up a batch of pancakes. I brought along pancake mix that comes in a plastic container and requires only adding a little water to make the batter. I don't burn the flapjacks, nor are they gooey and uncooked in their centers. It is a good start to the day.

We break camp, load the canoe, and paddle off into the morning in search of the 55-rod portage to Glee Lake. After a short paddle on Glee, we easily find the 25-rod portage to Fay Lake, which is about a mile long and has no campsites. At the end of Fay Lake, we continue paddling into the narrow Club River and War Club Lake. Then a short 15-rod portage into Seahorse Lake, which is at first more a narrow river than a lake. Paddling is relatively easy, although the day is becoming warmer, and I can feel sweat pouring down my back, underneath my ever-present life jacket. (Although I learned to swim

20

when I was a kid, I never step into a canoe or a boat without wearing a life jacket. It's my advice to all who canoe or boat. You just never know when you might find yourself in the water.)

From Seahorse Lake, indeed shaped like a sea horse, we find the 25-rod portage to French Lake and begin to feel a little cocky about our ease in finding portages. This will soon change.

Three-cornered French Lake is only 112 acres, but it's 130 feet deep and boasts both lake trout and yellow perch. Without any difficulty we find the 27-rod portage to Gillis Lake. Now we are no longer paddling in little lakes. Gillis is 570 acres and 180 feet deep and is home to lake trout, northern pike, and yellow perch. Seven campsites are located on the north and west sides of the lake, one of them on an island. Tall trees come down to the water's edge, and rocky outcroppings appear everywhere. Unfortunately for us, the lake's many bays and coves prove a considerable obstacle to finding the portage to Crooked Lake, where we intend to camp for the night. We explore the nooks and crannies of Gillis Lake for the better part of an hour before we find the nearly hidden entrance to the 90-rod Crooked Lake Portage. Once more our confidence in finding portages has been shattered.

Crooked Lake is well named. It has as many bays and coves as Gillis Lake, but it is a bit smaller than Gillis, about 300 acres, and much shallower, only 66 feet at its deepest. We quickly learn as we paddle in Crooked Lake, searching for one of six campsites (three of them on islands), that huge boulders lurk just beneath the surface, a considerable distance from shore in several places. I quickly move from landscape-gazing to boulder-watching, peering into the depths for a monster, canoe-busting boulder. Steve told me earlier that I should keep a keen look-out for underwater rocks when we are near shore, especially as we are rounding points of land that jut out into the lake. But in Crooked Lake, huge under-water rocks seem to appear anywhere and every-where. We paddle slowly and successfully without any collisions. I am thankful for the sunny day that makes gazing down into the water relatively easy.

We select a campsite with a view of an island directly across a narrow expanse of water. The camp-site is high on the rocks, facing mostly south. Today we made six portages for a total of 237 rods, about two-thirds as far as the previous day. Yet I feel like we've done more—especially since we exhausted an hour searching for one of the portages. I have to remind myself that the search was a pleasant paddle, even if we didn't know where we were going. Steve wasn't too concerned that we didn't quickly find the portage. Time for me to take a lesson from the younger generation.

We pitch the tent and spend the rest of the afternoon relaxing and munching on trail mix and enjoying lemonade, which I've made from lake water treated with a bacteria-killing product called Pota-ble Aqua. The lake water appears clear and clean—I can see 15 or more feet into it. Still, we know not to drink the water, no matter how clear it may look or how thirsty we may be. Invisible, stomach-upsetting bacteria lurk in even the clearest lake water. Potable Aqua leaves an aftertaste, but mixing the treated water with instant lemonade crystals results in a safe and tasty drink. And on a warm afternoon, lemonade is much appreciated. (In recent years we take the time to boil all our drinking water for a minimum of two minutes, which also does an excellent job of killing waterborne bacteria and other baddies.)

Wednesday, August 17, 1983. Midafternoon. Crooked Lake
Bright sunshine. Hot. We have no thermometer, but I'm guessing high 80s. I'm writing this while sitting on a log by the fire ring at our spectacular campsite. Even Steve, who doesn't comment much about these things, said this is one of the most attractive campsites he's seen. And he's seen a lot of them. For me this campsite is like one you see in an outdoors magazine, nature's beauty at its best. We're on a high jut of stony land, facing south toward a little island. A seagull rookery is about 100 rods down the shore from our campsite—seagulls are everywhere. We've also seen and heard several loons.

In the evening I cook up a batch of dried noodles with cheese and broccoli. Sounds a bit unappetizing, but after a day of paddling and portaging, it's a tasty and filling dinner. As a Depression-era farm boy, I learned to eat just about anything. No complaints, and the camp cook is still in the good graces of the crew.

Thursday, August 18, 1983. 7:00 AM. Crooked Lake
The sun is coming up over my left shoulder as I sit looking out over the lake and toward the island a short distance away. Crooked fingers of fog lift from the cool lake water. Today we will stay in camp, relaxing and reading. I look forward to it. My shoulders, arms, and back look forward to it as well.

23

A breeze from the south whispers into camp and creates a slight chop on the lake. So far this trip, we've had no wind; the lakes are glassy smooth, which makes for good canoeing. I sit here looking out at a rocky island a few hundred yards across the water from our campsite and simply enjoy the view. No great thoughts. No worries.

We spend the day relaxing, napping, and reading. When we tire of those strenuous activities, we climb into the canoe, paddle along shore, and fish. We catch nothing.

Thursday, August 18, 1983. Late afternoon. Crooked Lake
Just finished reading Huxley's Brave New World. *What a great book and what a place to read it. Reading Huxley showed me what too much organization and control can do, and why we need places like the Boundary Waters to remind us of another world, perhaps even braver than his, where nature is in charge and little is controlled and predictable.*

I'm amazed at how few people we've seen since we've been here; three canoes, that's it. For me this surely is one of the attractions of the place—no elbows in the ribs, so to speak. No loud talking, laughing, radios blaring, boom boxes booming. No truck and auto sound. No exhaust fumes. No motorboats roaring by.

I'm sitting on a rock while I write this. A strong southerly breeze shakes the branches of the spruce and birch trees at the campsite. Waves splash against the stones and rock the canoe, which is tied to a little cedar tree. A gentle, not unpleasant sound.

The campsite sits on a huge rock outcropping. Here and there tree roots snake across the surface of the rocks, searching for moisture and nutrients. Up the hill a bit from the campsite several trees have toppled, their shallow root systems no match for a fierce summer storm.

In midafternoon two canoes go by, in one two young men, in the other two young women with a young man sitting in the middle holding a map and pointing. From my brief encounters with other canoeists, I've noted the following: Every canoe has a map reader who spends as much time map reading as paddling and does a lot of pointing toward the direction of what might be a portage tucked around the corner or hidden behind a big boulder. All seem to be smiling.

The view from our campsite south and west across the lake includes conical spruce trees along the shores

In shallow topsoil, the roots of the giant trees at many campsites snake across the top of the ground, creating interesting patterns.

of the lake and a spruce-and-birch-covered island with lichen-covered rocks a few hundred yards from our campsite. The rocks at our campsite are enormous; likely the entire campsite is one huge black rock outcropping with cracks running this way and that in no apparent order.

Two items of convenience in our campsite: the official Forest Service fire grate, and the even more official Forest Service toilet. The first, surrounded by logs, looks out over the lake. The second, a couple hundred yards up the hill from the campsite, is mostly hidden in the deep underbrush, save for the well-trodden trail that leads to it. The toilet has no sides and no roof. It's merely a wooden box with a toilet ring on top parked over a pit that some poor soul had the privilege of digging. Serviceable, but a bit uncomfortable when the mosquitoes choose to feast on your exposed skin or it's pouring down rain. The view from the place is not too shabby, though, for from its elevated position you can look far out across the lake.

This evening's dinner menu consists of dried rice with chicken. Open pouch. Dump ingredients into a pot. Add two cups of boiling water. Stir well and let sit for ten minutes. Spoon onto plates and enjoy. Of course we begin our repast with cups of dried soup; I have vegetable and Steve has chicken noodle. We agree that the chicken must have walked past the processing plant while the soup was being made—no evidence that any chicken had ever gotten inside the place. We've run out of lemonade, so I mix up some Tang. There's no comparison with lemonade, which we've come to enjoy. Tang loses the

Our cooking kit has always included a good stove. We used this little Coleman stove the first years we camped in the BWCAW.

taste competition with orange juice, too. But it does have an ample supply of vitamin C—says so right on the plastic container. For dessert we have freeze-dried blueberry cobbler, bought at a sporting goods store. Not great.

It's been a hot and humid day. This evening, with the breeze gone, I expect mosquitoes, but so far, so good. After we finish washing the dishes and pull the food bag into a tree, I find a comfortable spot on a log facing the lake. Once more I write in my journal while my observations are fresh in my mind.

Thursday, August 18, 1983. Evening. Crooked Lake
What are my feelings about this place? Surely it's hard work portaging and paddling, with no conveniences at the end of the day. None whatever, except for the fire ring and an official US Forest Service outdoor toilet.

I'm surprised that one can still find a wilderness area such as this within a reasonable driving distance of Madison (and several other cities). I'm impressed with how untouched these lakes appear. I'm guessing they look about the same to me as they did to the voyageurs who came this way more than two hundred years ago. Cottages, fancy big houses, and condo developments surround so many lakes these days; not so here.

Since Steve left for college and has worked summers as a camp counselor, I've seen little of him. It's been a special treat to be with him for a few days. He's very quiet and seldom lets his feelings show. But it's clear he has a love for the outdoors, as do my other children.

I'm a little surprised that Steve never says he misses TV and music that seem to surround young people these days. A fringe benefit to canoeing with Steve is he carries the canoe and a pack at the same time. Oh, to be young again, and in shape. His camp counselor job requires that he be certified for Red Cross first aid and Red Cross lifesaving, a definite advantage in having him on the trip.

Not a breath of air this evening. The only sound is that of mosquitoes looking for dinner. I sleep on top of my sleeping bag, thankful that the tent's mesh mosquito-proof door and windows are keeping the bugs at bay but letting the air through. At 2 AM I am awakened when a huge clap of thunder shakes the ground under the tent. Lightning flashes so brightly that I can read my watch without digging for my flashlight. And then the booming thunder, clap after clap, before a gust of cool wind shakes the tent and the rain begins falling by the bucketful. I usually enjoy the sound of raindrops on canvas, but not when the rain falls in torrents while the wind threatens to pull out the tent pegs and flatten the tent. I crawl over and zip up the solid panels at the door and the windows.

Steve continues to sleep, apparently not hearing any of this. I shake his shoulder, and when his eyes open I ask, "What should we do?"

"About what?" he says sleepily.

"About the storm."

"Go back to sleep. Doesn't pay to worry when you can't do anything about what's happening."

I listen for the sound of the canoe rubbing against the rocks. I can't hear it. Has it torn loose and floated away? What would we do without a canoe, our only means of leaving this place?

I listen to the raindrops on the tent and decide that Steve is right. We'll worry about any consequences of the storm in the morning. I go back to sleep. With the first hint of dawn I feel around the inside of the tent and find a very wet shirt. Water has run into the tent—but not as much as I feared. Our sleeping bags have been spared.

We awaken to a cloudy, windy day, the last day of our trip. After a light breakfast—some trail mix, mostly—we pack our considerably wet gear in the canoe, and we are once more paddling. From Crooked Lake we portage 55 rods to Owl Lake. From Owl Lake we portage 63 rods to Tuscarora Lake. We begin paddling our way back to where we parked our car.

Tuscarora is an open lake of over 800 acres, 2 miles across and 120 feet deep. The west end of Tuscarora supports some of the oldest forest in the area, nearly two centuries old, stretching west to Owl Lake. But it is not a lake I want to canoe on a windy day. We find the portage to Missing Link Lake with little difficulty, but what a killer portage it is—366 rods, more than a mile, through lowland and marsh. It takes us an hour and a half to complete the portage. I'm glad we do it in the morning. It uses up about all the energy I have. After a short paddle across Missing Link Lake, a 42-rod portage to Round Lake, and an easy paddle to the boat landing, we complete our journey. We toss the wet gear in the back of the Horizon, hoist the canoe on top, and begin the long drive back to Madison.

This first trip to the Boundary Waters is one I will never forget. It will turn out to be a trip I will make every year. Each year adds something new to my collection of canoe stories; each trip gives me one more taste of wilderness life and all that it has to offer.

2

Foundations

In late summer of 1983, my son Steve had completed his work as a counselor at a youth camp and had a week off before starting the fall term as a photojournalism student at Winona State University in Minnesota. Steve asked me if I'd like to spend the week canoeing with him in northern Minnesota's Boundary Waters Canoe Area Wilderness. Steve and his younger brother, Jeff, and sister, Sue, had canoed the BWCAW several times with church groups and friends. I had heard their stories and was intrigued, but outside of an overnight canoe camping trip with Jeff on Wisconsin's Mecan River in the 1970s, I had never canoe camped. I had erroneously concluded that the BWCAW was for in-shape young people who enjoyed paddling long hours, didn't mind hiking untold distances on rock-strewn, usually hilly but sometimes marshy portages, and sat around campfires at night singing "Kumbaya" and other time-honored camping tunes.

Steve said, "Dad, I think you'll like it."

"But I'm not so young anymore." (I was forty-nine at the time.)

"Neither am I," Steve said, smiling. (He was twenty.)

I was a department chair at the University of Wisconsin in Madison and was feeling the pressures of trying to keep a fairly sizable university department on track, juggling the inevitable bickering that occurred among our twelve secretaries, the differing educational philosophies of our fifteen faculty members, and the often unfortunate competition among our graduate research assistants. I was ready for a break. I quickly said yes to Steve's offer.

Ruth and I have camped since we were first married (though never with a canoe), and we camped often while our three children were growing up. When I shared with her the plans Steve and I had to canoe camp in the Boundary Waters, she smiled and told me we should have a good time. She didn't say she wanted to join us.

That night, as I lay awake thinking about my upcoming trip to the Boundary Waters, I thought about my earliest camping experiences, which go back to my days in the US Army in the 1950s. We didn't call what we did camping, however. It was maneuvers, war games, or usually simply bivouacking.

In the summer of 1954, I was in army basic training stationed at Fort Eustis, Virginia. Part of that training included a week of bivouacking at what was then Camp A. P. Hill, a 76,000-acre training site 40 miles north of Richmond. For most of a day, my fellow recruits and I sat in the back of army trucks, bouncing our way toward an experience some of my fellow troopers feared more than anything we'd done so far. We had crawled through the mud under barbed wire with .50-caliber machine guns firing over us, marched 10 miles in the rain, and stumbled, run, jumped, climbed, and otherwise tried to negotiate obstacle courses. We had even listened to hours of mind-numbing lectures on military maneuvers. Now the raw fear of living in a tent in the woods was etched on the faces of my fellow recruits. But I was looking forward to it—anything to escape the spit and polish of barracks life, where a shoe not properly shined or a bunk improperly made led to demerits and loss of weekend leave time.

We arrived at the bivouac site in early evening and had about an hour to unload gear, set up our tents, and make ready for the night. We each carried a weapon, a .30-caliber M1 carbine, but no ammunition—a wise choice on the part of the army. The last thing I wanted was for my tentmate to have live ammunition in his state of fear. I teamed up with a frail-looking, wide-eyed chap from New York City named George. George was already scared out of his wits with the thought of sleeping in this little pup tent in the wilds of Virginia with only a piece of smelly olive drab separating him from the creatures of the night.

As we were still settling in, the sun dropped below the horizon and the Virginia woods quickly became the darkest place I'd been for some time. For some reason, no one had a flashlight—perhaps part of the army's strategy. For George, it was the darkest place he'd ever experienced, and he told me so. Several times.

"What creatures are out here?" he asked in a soft, shaking voice.

"I don't know," I answered. "But I'll bet they're more afraid of us than we are of them."

"You sure?"

"Go to sleep," I said.

"I can't. I hear something out there."

Our discussions went on for a couple hours as George fought his fear, holding his unloaded rifle in his hands.

"What's that sound on the tent?" he asked later, sounding even more alarmed than before.

"Sounds like raindrops to me."

"Only rain? Are you sure?"

"I'm sure. Go to sleep."

I drifted off to sleep thinking of the sound of raindrops on our barn roof when I was a kid. I liked the gentle drumming of rain on the canvas, a soothing sound that I enjoy to this day.

George and I both survived the night, of course. But he never let me forget how much he hated sleeping in a tent. Unlike most of my fellow officers in basic training, I put down bivouacking as the most interesting and enjoyable part of the experience. And I've been hooked on spending time in a tent and camping ever since.

My interest in nature and the environment goes back even further. Growing up on a central Wisconsin farm in the 1930s and 1940s provided me a first-hand introduction to the out-of-doors—and to dark nights, as we had no electricity on our farm until the late 1940s. My father, a lifelong farmer, was also a student of nature. He knew trees and wildflowers, birds and wild animals, their calls and their habits. And he was a hiker. On Sunday afternoons in all seasons of the year, we'd walk for miles across our farm and our neighbors' land. On those walks Dad taught me how to listen and look, how to walk quietly, and above all how to be patient, especially if I wanted to see wildlife. With my two brothers, we fished in summer and winter, and in fall and winter we hunted for wild game, an important part of our food supply in those Depression and World War II years.

My brothers and I attended a one-room country school, and part of our nature education was walking a mile each morning and night to and from school, from late August until late May, along a dirt-surfaced country road that had little or no traffic. We saw the seasons change, watched Canada geese fly over in spring and fall, saw winter snow become spring mud and then summer dust on our country road. We saw wild apple trees bud, flower, and in fall produce shiny red apples for the taking. Listening to *Afield with Ranger Mac,* a nature program broadcast by the University of Wisconsin station on our country school radio, added to my interest, as did enrolling in a 4-H forestry project at age eleven.

School also introduced me to the great outdoors writers. I first learned about Henry David Thoreau and his book *Walden,* published in 1854, in a high school English class. At the time I thought he was just another dead, difficult-to-read author. But over the years I have read and reread Thoreau's work. With each reading, I gain a new appreciation for this man who chose to live simply and to write about it.

I remember being introduced to Ralph Waldo Emerson during high school as well, when we discussed his 1841 essay on self-reliance. I didn't read Emerson's nature writing until much later; but when I did, I was especially taken with his 1836 essay

"Nature." His statement, "The lover of nature is he whose inward and outward senses are still truly adjusted to each other; who has retained the spirit of infancy even into the era of manhood,"[1] is one I often think about.

By the late 1950s, I was working as a camp counselor at a 4-H conservation camp, where I found a copy of *A Sand County Almanac* on the bookshelf in the main lodge. I found Aldo Leopold's ideas and his lyrical, storytelling way of writing intensely interesting. Once a University of Wisconsin–Madison professor, Leopold is credited with developing our modern-day ideas about environmental ethics and wilderness conservation. His message was clear, his writing elegant. He wrote, "Ability to see the cultural value of wilderness boils down, in the last analysis, to a question of intellectual humility. The shallow-minded modern who has lost his rootage in the land assumes that he has already discovered what is important."[2]

From Leopold I learned that a relationship with the land involves much more than hiking and identifying, more than wood chopping and tree planting. I learned that a true connection to the land requires thinking, feeling, and acting that comes from deep within and that can be cultivated and nurtured throughout a lifetime by hiking in the woods, taking time to watch a sunset, and, of course, canoeing in the Boundary Waters.

By the mid-1960s, I was writing a nature column for several central Wisconsin newspapers. While doing research for one of my columns, I found Sigurd Olson's books *Listening Point* and *The Singing*

Wilderness. Soon I was drawing on Olson's work, especially his philosophy that all of us are searching for ways to connect to nature and discover its deeper meaning in our lives. I also learned of Olson's efforts to preserve the Boundary Waters. In his book about the Boundary Waters, *The Singing Wilderness*, he wrote, "[The Singing Wilderness] is concerned with the simple joys, the timelessness and perspective found in a way of life that is close to the past."[3]

About the time I discovered Olson's writing, I also began reading John Muir. Muir, born in Scotland in 1838, spent his childhood years not far from my central Wisconsin farm. Today he is revered as the father of the National Park System. His book *The Story of My Boyhood and Youth* recounts his adventures on his family's little farm near Fountain Lake in Marquette County. Muir influenced my thinking about the importance of wilderness areas and the need to protect them. He also impressed on me that one person with strong beliefs and energy can make a difference.

Rachel Carson's book *Silent Spring* came out in 1962, when I was working as a University of Wisconsin extension agent in Green Bay. With her understandable, often lyrical writing style, Carson pointed out the devastating effect of DDT and other pesticides on the environment and influenced the return of the bald eagle and other bird populations that had suffered from pesticide poisoning in the 1950s and 1960s. *Silent Spring* evoked a storm of criticism, especially from pesticide manufacturers, and I was again reminded that taking a stand for nature and the environment could have its risks. Carson stood firm, and through her efforts, DDT was banned in the United States in 1972 and a new set of pesticide regulations emerged.

I eventually published two books based on my nature column. For the first, *The Land Still Lives*, I asked Gaylord Nelson, former Wisconsin governor, US senator, and founder of Earth Day, to write an introduction. I had long been impressed with Senator Nelson's commitment to improving the environment, and I was privileged to hear him speak at the University of Wisconsin–Madison Stock Pavilion on April 21, 1970. Nelson said, "[Earth Day] may be the birth date of a new American ethic that rejects the frontier philosophy that the continent was here for our plunder—an ethic that instead accepts the idea that even urbanizing, affluent, mobile societies such as ours are dependent on the fragile, but life-sustaining systems of the air, the water, the land. Such an ethic… will set new standards for progress, emphasizing human dignity and well-being rather than an endless parade of technology that produces more gadgets and waste and pollution."[4] Powerful words.

More recently I have become aware of Calvin Rutstrum's work. Having grown up in Minnesota's Twin Cities, Rutstrum sought a simpler, quieter life, spending much of his time away from the maelstrom of the city. Rutstrum was a storyteller, recounting in his books tales of canoeing, backpacking, conversations with Native Americans, and enjoying a life without the clutter of modern conveniences. He wrote about everything from the need for environmental preservation to the importance of solitude.

In *The Wilderness Life*, Rutstrum wrote about our place in nature: "As man hopes to exalt himself about all other creatures in the most ennobling sense, what perplexes is that he has not been able to adjust to the earth as well as most other creatures without seriously impoverishing it."[5] And further, "To have looked upon all life as *lower* than man, no doubt, is part of the ecological setback from which man now suffers."[6] One could conclude from Rutstrum's writing that a major reason for the environmental challenges the world faces is the erroneous and arrogant belief that humans are above and apart from the rest of nature. Spending time in a wilderness area such as the Boundary Waters could be a small step toward changing this belief.

And now, on my first planned trip to the Boundary Waters, I was once more looking forward to a week's immersion in nature, living with it and continuing to learn and appreciate.

I had not been in a true wilderness area before, although as a farm boy and farmer I had many encounters with nature. The Boundary Waters experience would be new for me.

A peaceful day in the Boundary Waters. A campsite is ahead on the right.

3

Provisioning

Steve and I had decided to leave for the Boundary Waters on Monday, August 15. The Friday before, we began provisioning for our trip. We had little time to round up the necessary equipment for a week in the wilderness with no Kmart or McDonald's close by if we forgot something.

Our family had been camping since the kids were little, and back in the early 1960s I had purchased a used umbrella tent, the kind with a substantial wooden pole in the center and a folding steel framework that forms an umbrella shape. It was old-fashioned green canvas, heavy (about 25 pounds), smelly, and it leaked, particularly the floor. We camped our way to Manitoba in 1967 with this tent and used it for several years at campsites around Wisconsin and at our farm in central Wisconsin. I knew the old tent well. It stood up in the fiercest storms, but our sleeping bags usually got wet.

"What about our tent?" I asked Steve.

"Too heavy for canoeing and portaging," he said with an air of someone who had carried heavy equipment on long portages. I had never portaged, so I had no idea how important it was to pay attention to weight—of every item you plan to carry. "Besides, it leaks," he added. Steve knew that old tent as well as I did.

Our neighbors in Madison, Jim and Marge, owned a four-person Eureka tent. Jim said, when I asked, "Sure, take our tent." It was a modern tent (at least in comparison to our heavy, green canvas umbrella shelter) made of ripstop nylon, with a rain fly. Jim assured us that neither bottom nor top would leak.

"How about our Coleman camp stove?" I asked. We had a green two-burner camp stove with a red fuel tank that had served us well over the years.

"Too heavy," Steve announced again.

"I don't think it weighs more than ten pounds," I said.

"Way too heavy," he said, dismissing the suggestion.

I started a list of things we needed to buy before we headed north on Monday. *Camp stove*, I wrote.

"What about our canoe?" I quietly asked, wondering if our old, sturdy 17-foot aluminum Grumman would pass muster. I'd bought the canoe in 1964, always stored it inside during the winter, and had only canoed on our 5-acre farm pond. It didn't have so much as a scratch on it, having never come in contact with a rock or even a gravelly beach. It weighed about 85 pounds.

"Canoe's fine," Steve pronounced. "Except, it has a part missing."

"Part missing?" I hadn't noticed any missing parts; it always seemed to work well.

"It doesn't have a yoke."

"A what?"

"A yoke for portaging. So you can carry it on your shoulders."

"Oh," I said, not wanting to admit that I didn't know a thing about canoe yokes. I wondered if it was similar to the yokes that oxen wore.

Canoe yoke, I wrote next on my list.

Portaging a canoe can be an onerous task, especially if the portage is long, the canoe is heavy, and the yoke is inadequate.

"We'll use the wooden canoe paddles we have, but we need a spare in case we break one."

"Did you ever break a canoe paddle?" I asked, wondering what kind of situations would result in a broken paddle.

"Not so far."

I wrote *canoe paddle* on my to-buy list.

"We have our aluminum cooking kit," I offered. Our mid-1960s nested kit included aluminum plates, a coffee pot, cooking pots, a skillet, and six coffee cups.

"Too heavy, but we'll use it," Steve said. "Don't forget your compass [I'd gotten one for my twelfth birthday], your waterproof match case, some mosquito repellent, and a couple flashlights. Bring along the first aid kit, too. The little one you have in the car."

I added the items to my list. "What about food? Aren't we supposed to be using some of that freeze-dried stuff they sell in the camping equipment stores?" I asked.

"It's okay, but it's kind of expensive. Dried food from the grocery store is just as good."

"How about bringing our ice chest, so we can have milk, cold beer, maybe some steaks?"

"Weight, Dad. Weight," Steve said, shaking his head. "Besides, what do we do when the ice melts after the first day?"

"Right," I said. I was thinking, *Do they make freeze-dried beer? I'm sure a cold one would go well after a hard day of canoeing.* But now I was dreaming.

Food was next on my list. We hadn't gotten into the specifics, except that Steve recited the official Boundary Waters camping rules. "No glass. No metal cans. Everything you bring in, you take out. Everything."

"Right," I said again. This was starting to sound complicated.

We discussed backpacks. I had my old army olive drab duffle bag.

"It'll do," Steve said. "Until you can buy something better." I didn't ask if he meant for this trip.

"Our sleeping bags and air mattresses?" I asked, pleased that I had thought of something important.

"Too heavy, but we'll use the ones we've got. Put garbage bags on your list. We stick everything in garbage bags. Keeps stuff dry if we dump."

"Dump?"

"Tip over. Swamp. Sink."

I was immediately reminded of life preservers.

"Bring a couple of those old, bulky orange life preservers, too." Steve's mind had gone in the same direction as mine.

"Clothes?"

"Don't need much. Change of underwear. Change of socks. I wear the same shirt and pants all week."

"You do?" I wanted to ask if his mother knew this but thought better of it.

"Ropes. We'll need some ropes to hang our food pack in a tree so the bears can't reach it."

"Bears?"

"Yup, bears can be a problem, Dad. A real problem."

"You ever see a bear in the Boundary Waters?"

"No. But you've got to be prepared. By the way, don't forget to bring your Swiss Army knife."

"I won't," I said, wondering what connection Steve saw between bears and Swiss Army knives.

Our first stop was the grocery store, where we bought a pound of Cheddar cheese, a 1-pound beef log, a couple of boxes of crackers, peanut butter in a plastic jar, strawberry jam (also in a plastic container) freeze-dried potatoes, freeze-dried beef Stroganoff, freeze-dried cheese and broccoli (which sounded terrible), a box of macaroni and cheese, dried instant soup, shake-and-pour pancake mix in plastic containers, three tubs of Tang, twelve containers of lemonade crystals to add to our treated water, and a box of super-tough garbage bags. We also bought a box of granola bars and a pound of trail mix made of dried fruit, nuts, and various mystery ingredients. Steve added a box of full-size Snickers bars to our cart.

Mealtime is a highlight of a wilderness experience. Appetites are sharp, and even a poor camp cook can be a hero.

"Can't canoe without Snickers bars," he said, smiling. "Keeps you going on the long portages."

We remembered toilet paper and film for our cameras, a box of sealable plastic bags, and a small plastic bottle of mosquito repellent.

"Lot of mosquitoes in Minnesota," Steve said.

We trekked off to a camping supply store, which also sold rifles and shotguns and fishing poles and lures. The camping equipment was tucked way in the back.

"Need a few things," I said to the young woman who asked how she could help.

We soon had a new Coleman single-burner camp stove, an aluminum fuel container, a gallon of Coleman fuel, a spanking-new wooden canoe paddle, 50 feet of $3/8$-inch rope, a canoe yoke, and a sack of freeze-dried blueberry cobbler.

How could we resist the cobbler, asked the attractive young woman who had been fluttering her eyelashes at Steve since she'd first encountered us. She gushed on and on about how we absolutely needed some of their freeze-dried food products for our trip. While she was selling Steve on the virtues of freeze-dried food, I was searching for some freeze-dried beer. It seemed like everything else was freeze-dried, why not beer?

Reservations are required for summer canoeing in the BWCAW and must be made several months ahead. Permits can then be picked up at ranger stations, like this one in Grand Marais, Minnesota.

4
_____

Long Drive

It's a long drive from the west side of Madison, Wisconsin, to the south side of Grand Marais, Minnesota, where our Boundary Waters permits waited for us. Four hundred thirty-nine miles, to be exact.

On Sunday afternoon, August 14, Steve and I stuffed our food, clothing, new stove, gasoline, and sleeping bags into garbage bags. "Just in case we dump," Steve said again. Then we stuffed the bulging garbage bags into my old army duffle bag, which was soon bursting at the seams. The canvas bag was heavy but strong, with shoulder carrying straps— which we would soon discover were not designed for long portages.

When we got home from the sporting goods store with our new canoe yoke, we discovered it was designed for a considerably wider model Grumman than ours. We called the store and learned it was the only yoke they carried. What to do? Even in 1983, folks knew about duct tape. I retrieved a big roll of it from a shelf in the garage and taped the yoke to where Steve thought it should go on the canoe. Because it was too big for our canoe, about 2 inches of menacing aluminum stuck out from each side of the canoe, something we'd have to keep in mind at all times when handling the craft.

In those days, I drove a 1980 Plymouth Horizon, a rather small car and certainly not one designed to have its innards packed full with camping equipment and a 17-foot aluminum canoe strapped to its top. The canoe stuck out several feet in both front and back of the car. In the 1980s, little cars like ours were considered an answer to the oil problems of the 1970s. The Horizon had a four-cylinder engine and got reasonably good gas mileage but had no power for climbing hills, doing off-road treks, or attempting similar challenges. But it would have to do.

I slept little that night, thinking of this new adventure and my first introduction to this "very special place," as some people called it. We were up before 5:00 AM and on the road by 5:30. The trip on the interstate highway to Eau Claire is a long three-and-a-half-hour drive but relatively easy, save for a headwind doing a number on our canoe and in turn on our little red car. The canoe shuddered with each gust of wind, and the Horizon shuddered in turn. Two hands on the wheel at all times. No relaxing to gaze at the rolling and attractive farm country we passed through.

At Eau Claire we left behind the interstate, with its heavy truck traffic and the shake and shudder we felt whenever a truck passed us—and they often did. We sputtered on, drawing every ounce of horsepower the little Plymouth's engine could muster. We stopped for gas ($1.25 per gallon) and then eased through Eau Claire, facing stoplight after stoplight after stoplight, and then struggled up to 55 miles per hour again on Highway 53 (which was under construction and would be for several years as road crews expanded it from two to four lanes).

We passed Chippewa Falls, home of regional favorite Leinenkugel beer. We passed Bloomer, New Auburn, and Chetek, and farmland slowly began disappearing as we entered Wisconsin's famed Northwoods. Then it was Cameron and Rice Lake as we drove on, taking turns at the wheel and searching for local radio stations that grew dim almost as soon as we tuned them in. We drove through Haugen, Sarona, and Spooner, a bit larger than the other cities. Up and down long, meandering hills with Northwoods vegetation invading the ditches—birch, pine, and spruce, black-eyed Susans and fireweed, and grasses turning brown as the summer days grew shorter and autumn lingered around the corner. Then it was Trego, Minong, Wascott, and Gordon, little towns where loggers once filled the saloons on Saturday nights, but where city-dwellers now flocked to the fishing lakes during the hot summer months. Finally we passed Solon Springs as we motored on, the Plymouth struggling under its heavy load and challenged by the long hills of the north. A short while later, as we crested one of those hills, we spotted far in the distance the waters of Lake Superior, a foggy haze hanging over its deep-blue surface.

Lake Superior, about the size of the state of Maine, is the largest freshwater lake in the world by surface area. About 350 miles long and 160 miles wide, it touches Michigan, Wisconsin, Minnesota, and Ontario, Canada. At a spot 40 miles north of Munising, Michigan, the lake is 1,300 feet deep. The

The shores of Lake Superior are rocky, rugged, and beautiful. This is a view of this largest of the Great Lakes from Grand Marais.

waters are dangerous to shipping, even with today's modern navigation equipment. Hundreds of ships have sunk here, the largest and most famous being the SS *Edmund Fitzgerald*, a 729-foot ore carrier that went down with twenty-nine crew members on November 10, 1975. The lake's cold temperature traps any drowning victims in its depths, so Superior has long been known "to never give up its dead." With an average annual temperature of 45 degrees Fahrenheit, the lake moderates the climate of the land it touches, making winters warmer and summers cooler than inland locations. The lake is also well known in winter for the lake effect that dumps up to 350 inches of snow on Michigan's Upper Peninsula and Wisconsin's far northeast.

The French explorer Étienne Brûlé is credited with being the first white person to see Lake Superior, in about 1620. Other French explorers and missionaries followed: Raymbault, des Groseilliers, Raddison, Ménard, Allouez, and Greysolon, to mention a few. These early French explorers named this big lake *le Lac Superieur*, "upper lake." The Ojibwa called the lake *Kitchi-Gummi*, meaning "great water" or "great lake." In his 1855 *Song of Hiawatha*, Henry Wadsworth Longfellow spelled the name a little differently but made it known to legions of school children, myself included.

> By the shores of Gitche Gumee,
> By the shining Big-Sea-Water,
> At the doorway of his wigwam,
> In the pleasant Summer morning,
> Hiawatha stood and waited.

We pulled into sleepy little Superior, population about thirty thousand in 1983. The once vibrant logging town, founded in 1854 and incorporated in 1889, is still a major shipping center snuggled against the lake, its climate largely dictated by the big water. We drove by oceangoing ships tied up near huge grain silos—the world coming to Superior, Wisconsin, via the Saint Lawrence Seaway, a linked set of locks and canals that opened in 1959 and connects the Great Lakes to the Atlantic Ocean. Across the big bridge, past views of more ships in port and others far out in the lake, steaming toward their destinations, and we arrived in Duluth. I was reminded of the time I was driving north from Minneapolis toward Duluth, where I was to teach summer school at the University of Minnesota–Duluth, and I passed a promotional sign along Highway 35, a big colorful one with large words shouting, Next to Duluth, we're Superior. When you know you've been exceeded, you take bold steps—especially if you are Superior's chamber of commerce. Duluth and Superior are in different states, of course, but also in different worlds, it seemed. There's nothing sleepy about Duluth, with its busy tourist attractions, its marine museum adjacent to the big lift bridge, and a host of restaurants and other downtown attractions in an area that had once been rather run down.

At about ninety thousand, Duluth's population in 1983 was about three times that of Superior's. The city traces its roots to the French explorers who traded with the Sioux and Ojibwa tribes here in the late 1600s. It is named for one of these French traders, Daniel Greysolon, Sieur du Lhut, who attempted to make peace between the Native American tribes with the hope of gaining trading and trapping rights.

By the mid-1800s, Duluth was one of the fastest growing cities in the United States and on track to becoming a large midwestern city. But alas, the stock market crash of 1873 dashed these hopes. The city did grow to about one hundred thousand people by 1900 and boasted a considerable number of millionaires, some of whose lakeside mansions we passed on our way north out of town in search of Highway 61.

After the fur trading era, Duluth became a major lumber shipping center, and then, with the discovery of iron ore in northeastern Minnesota, a steel town. Soon western wheat arrived by the trainload at Duluth, where it was stored in gigantic grain elevators, awaiting ocean shipment to distant world ports.

Steve and I bungled our way through Duluth to Highway 61, which according to the road map fronted the north shore of Lake Superior and would take us to Grand Marais. On the north side of Duluth, we pulled into a Hardee's for a sandwich and then soon headed northeast toward Two Harbors and Castle Danger, followed by the intersection with Highway 1, which shot off to the left, northwest toward Ely, another major entry point to the Boundary Waters. We continued on 61 along the lake, with its huge boulders and rugged terrain. When the road fronted the lake we saw waves splashing high in the afternoon breeze and blue water as far as we could see. We continued through Little Marais and Schroeder and Tofte, where the Sawbill Trail starts and then winds north toward the BWCAW. All along Highway 61 we marveled at one lake scene and yet another, at waterfalls tumbling down rock faces, hurrying toward the big lake. We arrived at Lutsen, famous for its ski hill and waterfront cabins.

As we motored on, we met the occasional south-bound car with a canoe strapped to its top. "Making room for us," Steve said, smiling. And when a canoe-carrying car passed us (which they did fairly often), his comment was, "Competition. Always competition." Finally, in the distance we spotted Grand Marais, the jumping-off place for our canoeing adventure.

Grand Marais, the jumping-off point for many who canoe the eastern section of the BWCAW, is a quiet but interesting town.

5

Grand Marais

We drove into Grand Marais around 3:30 PM on August 15, two road-weary travelers. It was my first time in this quaint little tourist town, with its popular Lake Superior harbor, coast guard station with lighthouse, and a mix of old and newer architecture. *Grand Marais*, meaning "grand marsh," is a misnomer, for there are no marshes in the area, grand or otherwise. What you immediately see is the harbor, with several sailboats at anchor, and a quiet town, at least at first glance.

Before our trip I had read about the history of Grand Marais. The town was a Native American village for years before the first Europeans arrived. The Ojibwa called Grand Marais *Kitchi-Bitobig*, "double body of water." John Jacob Astor of the American Fur Company built a small trading post here in 1823, and by 1834 the American Fur Company had established a commercial fishing operation. The company abandoned both of these endeavors in 1840. After the 1854 Treaty of La Pointe, the region opened to European settlement. This treaty, between the United States and the Superior and Mississippi Ojibwa, took effect in 1855 and ceded all the Ojibwa lands in northeastern Minnesota to the United States. In return, the Ojibwa retained hunting and fishing rights in the region. Several Indian reservations were also established as part of the treaty negotiation.

With European settlement, many Scandinavians moved into the area. Eventually the Europeans logged off much of the great forests in the region. They searched for iron deposits. They fished commercially. And the region was forever changed.

Walking around Grand Marais, I could almost feel its history, seeing in my mind's eye the little Indian village and later the fishermen and loggers, the miners, and the trappers at one time or another gathering in this place near the waters of Lake Superior.

The harbor in Grand Marais is one of my favorite places to visit. Both Steve and I enjoy watching the boats, especially sailboats navigating their way through the harbor's entrance into the calm waters. In the early 1880s, the US Army Corps of Engineers arrived in Grand Marais to construct a breakwater that would protect the harbor's entrance. A lighthouse, about 32 feet tall and on a wooden framework, was constructed on the east pier of the breakwater in 1885.[1] The breakwater and the new lighthouse with its foghorn made it much safer for sailors to find their way into Grand Marais' little harbor, a fact that today is much appreciated by recreational boaters.

By 1885, when Grand Marais undertook its first census, the town boasted 172 residents: 48 European Americans, 46 Native Americans, and 78 souls of mixed or unknown ancestry. A newspaper, the *Grand Marais Pioneer*, began publishing in 1891 (it later became the *Cook County News Herald*). By

1900, Grand Marais' population had increased to 308, and it was incorporated into a village in 1903. By the time of Steve's and my arrival there in 1983, Grand Marais' population was 1,280.

Road builders completed the first wagon road from Grand Marais to Duluth in 1899, a distance of some 110 miles of rocky outcroppings, steep hills, waterfalls, and dense forest. Eventually this would become the road Steve and I had been traveling for the past two and a half hours.

Before Grand Marais became a staging area for canoeists and a tourist center for others who wanted to spend time in this cool-weather place, lumbering was a major industry here. Grand Marais is also the last stop for groceries and other provisions for those entering Canada some 40 miles to the north.

We arrived at the Grand Marais Ranger Station at 3:30 PM and patiently listened to a forest ranger explain the Boundary Waters rules: Enter only at your designated entry point. Paddle wherever you want but follow the portage trails, camp at specified sites, and build campfires only in the provided cast-iron grates. Absolutely no cutting of live trees, stripping bark from a live birch, carrying in glass or metal containers, using a motor, or washing dishes too close to the lake. While the rules are informally presented, they are formally enforced. Breaking a rule is grounds for being asked to leave. (Today the rules are explained in a video that all visitors to the BWCAW must watch; they then take a brief quiz to make sure everyone understands what to do and not do.)

With all the rules clattering around in my head, the clerk handed me a permit for entry point 53,

Brant Lake; entry date, August 16. Steve and I drove to downtown Grand Marais and found a quirky little sports store called the Beaver House (with a giant muskie sticking out above its door) where we could purchase out-of-state fishing permits. From there it was a short walk to the Lake Superior Trading Post in search of maps. It took us some time to find the right map for our planned trip. Finally, we bought a Fisher map that showed area roads, entry points, campsites, and portages. Scale: 1 inch equals 1½ miles. The fine print on the bottom of the map read, "This map is not intended for navigational use and is not represented to be correct in every respect." I was immediately curious as to in which respects it was likely to be inaccurate. And what about that disclaimer about navigational use—weren't we planning to navigate the BWCAW lakes?

We walked around town, looking in store windows, gaping at the tourists, and guessing who might be canoeists. We hiked to the harbor and marveled at the size of some of the sailboats we saw there, bobbing and waiting for their sailor owners to take them out on the big water. We sat on the beach for a time, watching the gulls swoop and dive, calling their raucous calls and running ahead of waves that rolled in and receded. For a long time we simply sat quietly, listening to the gulls and the soft murmur of the waves lapping at the rocky beach.

Rather than look for a campsite near our entry point, I had contacted a colleague of mine from the University of Wisconsin who owned a rental property in downtown Grand Marias. We spent our first night there in comfort. No mosquitoes, no bears in camp. Real beds. A solid roof over our heads. (This would not be our experience on future trips, when we camped at one of the Forest Service–approved campsites the night before we entered the BWCAW.)

The famous Beaver House in downtown Grand Marais is a good place to stock up on "sure to catch" fishing lures.

Steve and I have stopped in Grand Marais every year since that first trip to buy fishing licenses and camping permits, but also to visit the town and note any changes. In 2009 we walked along Wisconsin Street, past the Attic Gift Shop, the Crooked Spoon Café and Sven & Ole's Pizza (Norwegian pizza?), the famous Beaver House at the corner of Wisconsin and Broadway, and Drury Lane Books, a neat little bookstore within a stone's throw of Lake Superior. We stopped in front of the "World's Best Donuts Shop," which was celebrating forty years of operation that year. A sign on the door stated, "Effective September 8: closed on Tuesdays and Wednesdays due to shortage of help. We may also be closing rest of the week. Shop early."

Of course the Lake Superior Trading Post is still there—a must-stop if for no other reason than to check the new camping equipment and the wonderful selection of north country clothing, including hats of every shape and personality (hats do have personalities). Our favorite eating spot generally before and always after a stay in the BWCAW is the Blue Water Café, at the corner of Wisconsin and First Avenue. After a week of eating camp cooking, drinking instant coffee, and missing eggs and bacon (I know we could have these items in camp, but we don't), the Blue Water Café is like an oasis to a traveling Bedouin. Their coffee is superb, their flapjacks outstanding, and there is always a cluster of old-timers discussing everything from what the president is doing wrong to where the fish are biting.

⚬

For our first trip, Steve and I were up before 6:00 AM on August 16. We ate breakfast at the more-than-a-little-quaint South of the Border Café (it was but a few miles to the Canadian border), where we feasted on eggs, bacon, greasy hash browns, and strong coffee. We were ready. At least, my mind said I was ready.

We turned the Horizon onto the famous Gunflint Trail. In the late 1870s, explorers carved out

The Blue Water Café, with Lake Superior a stone's throw away, is a great place, especially for breakfast. Every year we stop here on our way out of canoe country and feast on flapjacks and some of the best coffee in the North.

the first Gunflint Trail, following an ancient Indian footpath. Today the Gunflint Trail is a 57-mile paved highway (Highway 12) from Grand Marais to Saganaga Lake, on the Canadian border. The Gunflint Trail was completed to Gunflint Lake in 1893. Some ninety years later we drove the same road from Grand Marais to our canoe launch site.

I noticed on our newly purchased map that the Gunflint Trail does not take you directly through the Boundary Waters Canoe Area Wilderness, but rather skirts one part of it to the east and north and cuts southwest of the northeast segment. I hadn't realized until then that the BWCAW was not all of one piece.

It was a peaceful early morning drive, up and down hills, through fog-shrouded valleys, past logging operations, across little streams, through dense forestland and occasionally past a sign for a resort or an outfitter. From all the publicity about the Boundary Waters and its connection to Grand Marais, you'd think the BWCAW was just down the road from the city, maybe a five-minute drive. Not so. We drove 48 miles along the Gunflint Trail until we came to County Road 47 and a sign pointing left to Tuscarora Lodge. From there it was three-quarters of a mile to Forest Route 1495. We turned right and followed this narrow road for about a mile, which brought us to a parking lot in the woods and a short hike down a hill to Round Lake, where we would launch our canoe.

The drive along the Gunflint Trail took about an hour and a half. For the first several miles I was uneasy about how slow we were going, until it hit me that we were here to relax. Time spent meandering down an interesting road should be savored as much as time in a canoe, I reminded myself. In our busy world, most of us spend far too much time focusing on our destinations and far too little time paying attention to the trip itself.

And we still weren't in the Boundary Waters.

The Gunflint Trail, a long and fascinating road through the BWCAW, leads canoeists to several entry points.

6

A Brief History of the BWCAW

As Steve and I launched our canoe into Round Lake, we were getting close to the Boundary Waters, but we still had a couple of portages and considerable paddling before we could finally say, "We have arrived."

The Boundary Waters Canoe Area Wilderness, located within northern Minnesota's Superior National Forest, encompasses 1,029,000 acres.[1] One might expect that the BWCAW would be administered by the US National Park Service, part of the Department of the Interior. In fact, the US Forest Service, under the US Department of Agriculture, runs the show. There are no park rangers in the BWCAW. You'll see forest rangers, if you're lucky. In the more than twenty-five years we've canoed the Boundary Waters, other than at ranger stations, we've seen forest rangers perhaps three times, checking on our equipment and making sure our permits were in order.

The BWCAW extends about 110 miles along the Canadian border from west of Hovland, Minnesota, to beyond Ely. It's about 30 miles across at its widest. Today the BWCAW includes 1,500 miles of canoe routes, about 2,200 designated campsites, and more than 1,000 lakes and streams.[2] About 75 percent of those lakes are reserved for nonmotorized travel. The BWCAW is adjacent to Canada's huge Quetico Provincial Park to the north. It's one of those interesting places where the international border often cuts across a lake. You can canoe here and truly not know what country you are in.

Knowing something about the geologic history of northern Minnesota helps us understand, at least a little, what makes the Boundary Waters so interesting and attractive. According to geologists, the BWCAW is positioned at the lower portion of the Canadian Shield, a huge region of granite bedrock covering more than 3 million square miles of Canada and northern North America. Up until about ten thousand years ago, and for several million years before that, vast glaciers pushed over the area, gouging and reshaping and creating the landscape we see today. These rock outcroppings contribute immeasurably to the beauty of the area.[3]

Following the glacier's retreat about ten thousand years ago, Native Americans migrated into the area, hunting, fishing, and gathering wild rice and other crops. By the mid-1600s, French traders began exploring the area, and in 1670 the English-owned Hudson's Bay Company was established, by charter the only company allowed to trade in the region at the time. The company soon had trading posts in various places on Hudson Bay. By the mid-1700s, French explorers pushed their trading network well into the western Great Lakes. French control of the trading network ended in 1763 when France ceded

Canada to the English as the result of the Seven Years' War. In 1784, the powerful North West Company, with headquarters in Montreal, emerged as major competitors for Hudson's Bay Company. The North West Company employed the famed voyageurs (the *coureur de bois,* or "runners of the woods") to haul by canoe tons of furs and mountains of trade goods used to barter with Native Americans. Europeans prized the lush furs trapped in the north of this country and Canada—the otter and lynx, the marten, and especially the beaver. Beaver hats were in high demand and beaver hides a valuable commodity. Trappers nearly wiped out the area's beaver population during the years from 1784 to 1821.[4]

Most of the voyageurs were French Canadian, although a considerable number were mixed blood (or métis), as the French Canadian and European traders often had First Nations wives or mistresses. From reading accounts of these heroic canoeists, one would expect them to be men of gigantic proportions. They were not. The average voyageur was five foot six, and few were taller than five foot eight. The trading companies employed short, stocky men because the taller ones took up too much room in a canoe. Although they may have been short, these men were strong, able to paddle fifteen to eighteen hours a day and carry enormous loads of merchandise on their backs over rocky portages, often at a pace that challenged travelers without loads to keep up.[5]

The voyageurs paddled two major types of birch-bark canoes, the north canoe (*canot du nord*), and the Montreal canoe (*canot du Maitre*). The north canoe was about 25 feet long, manned by six to eight voyageurs, and could carry about a ton and a half of cargo—mostly furs and personal possessions. It was light enough that two men could carry it. The Montreal canoe was considerably larger than the north, 35 to 40 feet long and 6 feet wide. Up to fourteen voyageurs paddled it, often across miles of dangerous open water on the Great Lakes. The Montreal canoe weighed more than 600 pounds when empty and could carry 4 tons of cargo.[6]

The voyageurs left Montreal when the ice went out in the spring, paddling west as far as the Great Lakes and sometimes beyond. Their traveling diet often consisted of pea soup, corn mush, and pork fat. The canoeists generally ate just two meals a day, breaking camp before daybreak, paddling until sunrise, and then stopping for breakfast. After breakfast they would paddle and portage all day, stopping in the evening to eat once more and sleep. They paddled rapidly, forty to sixty strokes a minutes.[7]

Grand Portage on Lake Superior (in what is now Minnesota) was the destination for the big Montreal canoes. There the voyageurs unloaded the manufactured trade goods and reloaded the Montreal canoes with furs from the wilderness for the return trip east. Western voyageurs wintered at Fort Chipewyan, on Lake Athabasca in the northwest corner of present-day Saskatchewan and the northeast corner of present-day Alberta. Eastern voyageurs wintered in Montreal. Every June or July, depending on the weather, the eastern voyageurs met the western voyageurs at Grand Portage, where they enjoyed a great celebration.[8] From 1784 to 1802, Grand Portage was the summer gathering place for North

West Company clerks and traders and as many as a thousand voyageurs, who danced, drank, feasted, and sang as well as competed against each other in various games such as wrestling and canoe racing. Then, with their big canoes loaded with furs the eastern group paddled toward Montreal, and the western group once more returned to the hinterland for the long winter soon to come.[9] On quiet nights while camping in the BWCAW, one can almost hear the lusty songs of the voyageurs who are so much a part of the Upper Midwest's story and myth.

After the Ojibwa signed the Treaty of La Pointe in 1854, much of eastern Minnesota and the area that became known as the Arrowhead Region belonged to the US government. The entire region was open to settlement, exploration, and exploitation by whites. Mineral prospectors rushed in seeking gold and eventually finding iron ore on the Vermilion Range, southeast of Ely. In the late 1800s and continuing to the late 1920s, the area was heavily logged. Several forest fires decimated the area during this time. The present day regrowth of tree species consists of jack pine, spruce, balsam, and aspen rather than the red and white pine and white spruce that grew here earlier (some old-growth pine can still be found in the area, spared by both loggers and fires).

In 1902, with the encouragement of Minnesota's chief fire warden, Christopher C. Andrews, the commissioner of the General Land Office withdrew half a million acres of forestland in Lake and Cook counties from entry, protecting the land from settlement or other development. In 1905 another 141,000 acres were withdrawn.

Then in 1909, President Theodore Roosevelt signed legislation setting aside a little more than 1 million acres (including the previously withdrawn acres) to create Superior National Forest. A few weeks earlier in that same year, Canada created Quetico Provincial Forest Reserve. This might be marked as the beginning of the BWCAW, although it would be several years before wilderness canoeing became a popular recreational activity.[10]

In 1912, presidential proclamation number 1215, signed by President William Howard Taft, added another 380,000 acres to Superior National Forest. In 1919, the US Forest Service hired landscape architect Arthur Carhart to develop a recreational plan for the country's national forests. Among his several recommendations, Carhart suggested that Superior National Forest emphasize wilderness canoeing. It was the country's first plan to manage and protect a wilderness area, but it was never implemented—obviously, an idea ahead of its time.[11]

Meanwhile, facing considerable local pressure in the 1920s to log Superior National Forest, the Forest Service developed an elaborate road-building plan. The Izaak Walton League of America publicly spoke out against the plan, helping to scuttle it. In 1926, US Secretary of Agriculture William Jardine designated a large part, "not less than 1,000 square miles," of Superior National Forest for wilderness recreation. This would become the nucleus of the Boundary Waters.

Still, with the growing popularity of automobiles and the American thirst for adventure and good fishing lakes, the pressure to develop Superior

National Forest land and the boundary lakes area only increased. Local governments, seeing tax dollars dancing in front of their eyes, pushed development ideas, including advocating "a road to every lake." Workers completed the 25-mile, mostly gravel Sawbill Trail, stretching from Tofte to Sawbill Lake, in 1931.[12]

By the mid-1920s, businessmen had their eyes on the region's waterpower potential, proposing to build as many as seven dams on rivers and streams that connected several Boundary Waters lakes, with the potential for raising water levels and significantly changing the area forever. After a five-year battle led by conservationist Ernest Oberholtzer and several others, the plan was killed.[13] In 1926, the Forest Service designated 640,000 acres in Superior National Forest as a roadless area, finally putting the kibosh on the "road to every lake" plan.[14]

In 1927, President Calvin Coolidge added another 360,000 acres to Superior National Forest.[15]

Two major logging eras affected the area. From 1895 to 1930, loggers cut the red and white pine that proliferated throughout the region, removing most of the old-growth timber. New trees emerged after the logging, but these were aspen and birch and other species that grow when the red and white pines are clear-cut. The so-called pulpwood logging era (1935–1938) resulted in the cutting of white cedar, birch, spruce, balsam fir, and jack pine over much of what is now BWCAW land. With these trees removed, the once pristine forest appeared naked, with little growing except newly sprouting trees and shrubs.[16]

In 1930, Congress passed the Shipstead-Newton-Nolan Act, which prohibited logging within 400 feet of lakeshores and prevented building dams in the area.[17]

During the years 1933 through 1942, the Civilian Conservation Corps brought more than 2,500 unemployed young men to the area. They planted trees, built canoe rests, and constructed many of the portage routes traveled by today's canoeists.[18] When Steve and I first began canoeing the BWCAW, we especially appreciated the canoe rests (a wooden framework where you can lean a canoe) while we caught our breath before slogging on during a long portage.

In the mid-1940s the area was called the Superior Roadless Area. Resorts on lakes without roads became popular as fly-in destinations. With seaplanes filling the air with their cargoes of fishermen, the area was quickly transformed into something that was far from wilderness. Sigurd Olson of Ely, Minnesota, a longtime environmentalist and well-known nature writer, and others took their complaints about the air traffic in the wilds to Washington. The Thye-Blatnik Act, passed in 1948, authorized the purchase of landlocked resorts in the Roadless Area, and in 1949 President Truman signed an executive order stating that aircraft could not fly below 4,000 feet, except for emergencies, in the Roadless Area, which prevented floatplanes from landing. The law went into effect in 1951. Lacking adequate funding and condemnation authority, some of these landlocked properties remained under private ownership until the 1960s.[19]

Starting in the late 1940s and continuing into the early 1960s, a series of laws passed by Congress made money available for the Forest Service to acquire private lands within the Roadless Area.

Local government officials spoke loudly against this private land acquisition, arguing it would once more decrease their tax base. Meanwhile, logging and the building of logging roads continued in Superior National Forest. In 1958 the Forest Service, recognizing that the maze of logging roads in the area contradicted the title Roadless Area, changed the name to Boundary Waters Canoe Area.[20]

You know you've arrived when you see this sign.

With aluminum canoes becoming widely available in the 1950s, canoe traffic in the BWCA increased dramatically. (In 1971 a Forest Service rule would limit visitors in the BWCA to designated campsites on "heavily used routes" and prohibit cans and glass bottles. The designated campsite rule would be extended to all areas of the BWCA in 1975.)[21]

With increased pressure by canoeists wanting to visit the BWCA and the ever-present business community pressing for more private development in the area, the future of the Boundary Waters was tenuous. It became obvious that additional legislation to protect the area was necessary.

Sigurd Olson helped draft the Wilderness Act of 1964 and worked with Minnesota senator Hubert Humphrey to assure its passage. Section 2(a) reads:

> In order to assure that an increasing population, accompanied by expanding settlement and growing mechanization, does not occupy and modify all areas within the United States and its possessions, leaving no lands designated for preservation and protection in their natural condition, it is hereby declared to be the policy of the Congress to secure for the American people of present and future generations the benefits of an enduring resource of wilderness. For this purpose there is hereby established a National Wilderness Preservation System to be composed of federally owned areas designated by Congress as "wilderness areas," and these shall be administered for the use and enjoyment of the American people in such manner as will leave them unimpaired for future use and enjoyment as wilderness, and so as to provide for the protection of these areas, the preservation of their wilderness character, and for the gathering and dissemination of information regarding their use and enjoyment as wilderness.[22]

This legislation designated the Boundary Waters Canoe Area as a unit of the National Wilderness Preservation System and recognized the unique history and character of the area.

Attempting to strike a compromise between those who wanted full protection of the Boundary Waters Canoe Area and many northeastern Minnesota citizens who resented both federal meddling with "their" land and the loss of jobs in logging, fishing, and snowmobiling, Senator Humphrey included continued logging and motor use in the legislation. These concessions to the citizens of northeastern Minnesota would prove to be flash points for years to come. The debate continued into the 1970s: Should the Boundary Waters Canoe Area remain open for a wide array of recreational and commercial uses, including motorboating, snowmobiling, and commercial logging? Or should the Forest Service manage the area as hands-off wilderness?

Debates, protests, newspaper editorials, and much gnashing of teeth occurred during the mid-1970s. Fundamentally, the issue revolved around the basic questions: Of what value is a wilderness area? And to whom? For many, value was expressed in monetary terms: jobs, income from fishing, bait sales, timber sales, cabin rentals, and so on. But to many others involved in the discussion, *value* meant something more difficult to describe, something that went well beyond money to the deeper needs of human beings who want solitude and the opportunity to connect with nature that often is only possible in a wilderness.[23]

Of course, the idea of the federal government interfering in local concerns infuriated many

Minnesota citizens. Earlier legislation—the no-fly ban and the closing down of landlocked resorts—had tossed gasoline on the increasingly hot issue of land use in the Boundary Waters Canoe Area. Locals simply couldn't stomach the idea that the Boundary Waters Canoe Area was a federal property and thus belonged to all the people of the United States.

After years of wrangling and the hard work of people like Sigurd Olson, Miron L. Heinselman, and many others, President Jimmy Carter signed the BWCA bill on October 21, 1978 (Public Law 95-495). The Boundary Waters Canoe Area was now officially known as the Boundary Waters Canoe Area Wilderness (BWCAW).

Section 3 of that act stipulated the following:

> The areas generally depicted as wilderness on the map entitled "Boundary Waters Canoe Area Wilderness and Boundary Waters Canoe Area Mining Protection Area" dated September 1978, comprising approximately one million and seventy-five thousand five hundred acres, are hereby designated as the Boundary Waters Canoe Area Wilderness (hereinafter referred to as the "wilderness"). Such designation shall supersede the designation of the Boundary Waters Canoe Area under section 3(a) of the Wilderness Act (78 Stat. 890) and such map shall supersede the map on file pursuant to such section.[24]

The act banned logging and mining, limited motorboats and the size of their motors, and essentially banned snowmobile use. Of the one thousand lakes and streams in the BWCAW, only fourteen allow motorboats.

Today, the Boundary Waters Canoe Area Wilderness is one of the largest and still quite easily accessible wilderness areas in the world, and more than 250,000 visitors find their way here from all parts of the country and around the world. Like many of those visitors, I look forward to my annual trip to the BWCAW with great anticipation.

An afternoon nap after a hard day of reading and resting.

Part II: Memories

Cold night weighs down the forest bough,
Strange shapes go flitting through the gloom.
But see—a spark, a flame, and now
The wilderness is home.

—Edwin L. Sabin, in *Camping and Woodcraft*
by Horace Kephart

As the sun goes down, a campfire takes the chill from the night air and provides a focal point for storytelling.

7

Campfires

A campfire on a chilly evening on the banks of a Boundary Waters lake brings warmth to my body and joy to my soul. A campfire does so much more than provide a source of heat and a little light on a dark evening when clouds hide the stars and darkness envelops our campsite. A campfire beckons to me, reminding me of my past and of those who have come before me.

I grew up in a home heated by woodstoves, one in the kitchen and one in the dining room. During the long, cold Wisconsin winters, we closed off the rest of the house and lived in these woodstove-heated rooms. I still heat my farm cabin with one. A woodstove is but one step away from a campfire. The flame is there, licking at the wood, and so is the smoke.

My dad and I spent many hours "making wood," as we called it, sawing down trees for our ever-hungry woodstoves. Sometimes with the help of a hired man, we made wood on days when the temperature was near freezing and on days when it was well below zero. Making wood was hard work. But it had its pleasant moments, too, particularly the campfire my dad always built when we made wood.

On the bitterly cold days it warmed us—and when we brought sandwiches with us for lunch, it toasted the sandwiches, too. But Dad also built a campfire on the days when the temperature was moderate, when we didn't really need one. Pa liked campfires, too, beyond the practical reasons for having one. He never talked about this, but I could see it in his eyes as he rubbed his bare hands over the open flame. He enjoyed a campfire for what it was, not only for what it could do.

We went ice fishing every winter weekend when I was a kid, on small lakes in central Wisconsin where in those days it was still possible to build a campfire on shore while we watched our tip-ups on the lake to see if we had a bite.

My dad, my two brothers, and I, and often one or more uncles, spent hours sitting by little smoky campfires, keeping warm and, more importantly, telling stories. A campfire was often the trigger to start the "I remember when..." sharing, with each story prompting another, and yet another. A campfire encourages storytelling, for it brings people close together and for some mysterious and unknown reason seems to draw out memories. The stories I heard on those many ice fishing forays, many repeated again and again, sometimes embellished a little or a lot, taught me much about storytelling and the power of a story in relating history.

Years later, when I was teaching at the University of Wisconsin–Madison, I led a group of workshop participants on a canoe camping trip from the Garrison Dam, on the Missouri River in North Dakota, to Bismarck. We were studying the Mandan

Indian culture as well as learning about the Lewis and Clark Expedition that had traveled the very route we canoed, but in the opposite direction. Each evening we camped at one of the Lewis and Clark campsites (many are now parks along the river), set up our tents, and built a campfire. I had even hired a Mandan shaman to travel with us.

After our evening meal, we gathered around the campfire and listened while the shaman told the creation stories of his tribe. He was regaled in buckskins and stood with his back to the river with the flames from the campfire lighting his face. There was a full moon that week, and it rose behind him as he talked. The campfire was essential to the atmosphere, with moonlight streaking through the tops of the trees and no sound but the river and the crackling of firewood. It was an experience that none of us will forget.

Now, as I sit by a campfire built in an official Boundary Waters fire grate, I think about campfires I have known over the years, and I allow my mind to consider what it must have been like on the banks of these lakes years ago, when the first explorers came this way, lugging their heavy canoes and stopping for the night to eat and rest—and, I'm sure, tell stories.

Over the years I have learned a considerable bit about making campfires. Occasionally a previous camper will have left a small pile of firewood—a kind of present from the previous occupant. I try to do the same. I have also discovered that when campfires are allowed (in very dry years the Forest Service bans them), the amount of available firewood in the vicinity of a campsite can be almost nonexistent. Campers who have come before us have already burned everything that was handy. What to do? When we are out in our canoes we look for driftwood washed up on the beaches. Of course, never, never cut a live tree near your campsite. This is a cardinal sin, not to mention a serious violation of Forest Service rules.

Starting a campfire can be one of life's most satisfying moments, especially if you are surrounded with campers who doubt your fire-making skills. I use windproof, waterproof matches. Trying to light a campfire in a stiff wind is practically impossible with ordinary kitchen matches, even worse with the little, wimpy-flamed matches that come in a box and that you strike on the side. The goal, of course, is to light a fire with one match. (Using two or more matches means failure and will evoke the scorn of your fellow campers.) The key to it all is constructing the campfire carefully before lighting it. Start with a piece of paper, or better still, a small piece of dried birch bark that you've found on the ground. (Remember, never strip birch bark from a live tree.) A birch that is dead and down is a fire-building prize for those who know the magic of a small piece of the white bark.

After the paper or birch bark, add a few small twigs (make sure they are dry), and then a few larger ones, and one or two larger still. Then, when all is ready and your confidence is high, kneel with your back to the wind, strike the match, touch it to the crumpled paper or birch bark, and watch your campfire come to life.

Once the fire is going, maintaining it is relatively easy, but a campfire is not to be ignored. Adding a stick of wood now and again, in the midst of a good story, often serves doubly—building suspense for the tale you are spinning, and of course keeping the fire perking along.

A campfire, a good book, and the sounds of the wilderness in the background. It's about as good as it gets.

8

Wilderness Sounds

As outdoors writer Ted Trueblood has said, "The silence of nature is very real. It surrounds you... you can feel it." When we camp in the Boundary Waters, we leave behind the hustle and bustle of daily life, with its sounds of sirens, construction equipment—the annoying *beep, beep* of a truck backing up—cell phones going off, TV sets blaring, radio programs, Internet noises, loud, talking people. Today's world is a noisy world, so noisy that for some people the sounds of silence are overwhelming, disturbing, and not to be tolerated. One year, when Steve's friend Rick, a police officer, camped with us, he brought along his portable CD player (these were the days before iPods). I didn't say anything, but Steve did: "No CD players in the Boundary Waters." There was no "Please put it away," no gentle reminder. A plain and simple message. Rick tucked the player away, and that was the end of the discussion.

Having said all this, let me quickly point out that the Boundary Waters is not a place without sound. Indeed not. The sounds are all around. But they are the sounds that belong here, that are of this place.

Sounds that add to the mystery and mystique of this vast wilderness.

I suspect the signature sound most associated with the Boundary Waters is the call of the loon. That eerie, primitive call in its many forms floats across the lakes, often hangs in the night air, and sometimes even serves as an alarm clock on a foggy morning. I say to my friends who ask why I keep returning to the Boundary Waters each year: "It's the call of the loon." I need to hear the loon's call at least once a year to be right with the world, to face the everyday challenges of life for another twelve months.

Plan for cold, windy days—and enjoy them, by remembering to bring along warm wind- and rainproof gear.

I also enjoy the sound of the wind. I don't know why I should be so enthralled by the wind, because I can't see it. But I can feel it, I can see what it does, and I have great respect for it. During most of the year, I don't pay much attention to the wind. But the wind in the Boundary Waters is a force to contend with. When canoeing, the wind can be both enemy and friend. It can kick up waves so high that one dare not venture out with the canoe for fear of swamping. At the same time, it can blow away a swarm of mosquitoes and make life in camp considerably more comfortable than it is on a calm, windless day during bug season.

I enjoy listening to the wind in the tops of the trees in the early fall, a moaning, mysterious sound that triggers memories of when I was a kid on the farm and the wind rustled the treetops in the woods just back of our farmhouse, creating sometimes soothing but often frightening sounds, depending on the wind's intensity. As I listen to the wind, I listen for the variety of messages the trees share: the soft sough of the white pine, its needles gently shaking; the gentle murmuring of white cedar branches; the nervous chatter of the aspen leaves as they shake and shudder; the death rattle of dead oak leaves clinging to a tree in winter. When the wind is high, the tree sounds all meld together in a low roar of protest.

When I'm snug in my tent on a windy Boundary Waters night, I enjoy this cacophony of sounds—the wind in the trees, the waves slapping against the rocks in rhythmic order, and the gentle protest of my fragile tent walls as they sigh and gently shudder. And I sleep soundly.

Thursday, September 4, 2003. John Lake
Yesterday, wind.
Wind from the north.
Wind sending waves crashing on rocks.
Wind snapping the cooking tarp.
Wind sending me in search of more clothing.
Wind turning my face red.
Wind keeping the canoe on shore.
Wind stopping all fishing.
Wind, invisible but so powerful.
This morning I sit facing east, waiting for the sunrise.
The sky is clear.
The wind is gone.

A couple of years ago I was sleeping soundly in my tent at our campsite on John Lake when I was awakened by what I thought was the sound of rifle shot, a sound I had never heard while canoeing in the Boundary Waters. I was instantly awake, fumbling for my flashlight. I unzipped my tent and stumbled out into the moonlit night. No sounds at all greeted me. The wind was down and fingers of mist rose from the warm lake water, colliding with the cooler night air.

I turned off the flashlight and gazed out onto the lake in the direction I thought the sound had come from. I heard it again, louder and clearer, a riflelike report that seemed to roll across the lake. Then I saw the source of the sound swimming just a few yards from our campsite: a huge beaver had slapped its big wide tail on the water. Earlier we had seen a spot where beavers were working along the shore, chewing off small aspen, but we had not seen them—beavers are mostly nocturnal, preferring to work when the rest of us sleep. Slapping its tail on the water is the beaver's alarm mechanism, to let other beavers know that danger may be near. I couldn't detect what was bothering this beaver. Perhaps it was our campsite and the few wisps of smoke rising from the nearly dead coals of our campfire. Or maybe, as Steve said later, "The beaver heard you snoring."

Other night sounds in the Boundary Waters have intrigued and fascinated me.

Thursday, September 5, 2002. Pine Lake
Heard a pair of owls calling to each other last night with the growl of thunder in the background. Owl calls and thunder sounds mixing together and echoing across the lake. Eerie. Owls making love calls? Likely. "Come to my place." "No, come to mine." This went on for nearly a half hour and then, as the rumble of thunder grew louder, the owls quit calling. Waiting for the rain?

I enjoy the sounds of waves slapping against the rocks below our campsite, gentle when the breeze off the lake is slight, violent when the wind comes up and takes charge. And I find nothing quite as relaxing as raindrops on my tent roof, especially at the beginning of a thunderstorm, as every raindrop is accounted for on the tent roof. It is like sitting inside a drum with the drummer beginning the tune slowly and then warming up, until the tent is filled with the sound of the rain beating to an ancient tune. As I listen to the rain, I think about the Native Americans, the voyageurs, the trappers and traders, the explorers, and then the canoeists like Steve and me who have been coming here year after year. I wonder if those earlier visitors enjoyed the sound of raindrops on their shelters, as we do.

The roar of thunder, causing fear and trepidation in many folks, is a joyous, wonderful sound to me. My love of thunder perhaps traces back to my days growing up on a sandy central Wisconsin farm where we never had enough rain. The sound of thunder rumbling in the distance usually forecast rain. As farmers, we needed rain, and we celebrated the thunder that announced its coming.

In the quiet of the Boundary Waters, the first low growls of thunder in the southwest often belie the fury of the storm to come. The clash of cool air from Canada colliding with warmer air from the south often results in violent, earth-shaking storms with torrents of rain, crashing thunder, and impressive lightning.

The many sounds of the wilderness bring us to the north each summer, reminding us how beautiful and exciting nature sounds can be when they're not masked by the noise of civilization.

To avoid mosquitoes, select a campsite that is open and faces south or
southwest to allow access to a mosquito-chasing breeze.

9

Bears

"Look out for the bears," my neighbor said, when I told him Steve and I had planned a canoe trip to the Boundary Waters. He was only half joking; he had grown up on a farm in northern Minnesota and had some experiences with bears.

When Steve and I picked up our permits at the Grand Marais ranger station in August 1983, the ranger said, in a very matter-of-fact way, "We've had a little bear trouble in the area where you're going." That offhand statement caught my attention much more than the litany of what we could do and not do, bring and not bring, on our excursion. I had absolutely no experience with bears—in fact, I had seen one only once in the wild, and that was when a bear crossed the highway in front of me as I was driving in northern Wisconsin at dusk one fall evening. I had thought it was a big dog until I looked more closely. It was not a dog.

"What kind of bear trouble?" I asked, trying to be nonchalant, like bear trouble could be expected in the usual run of things.

"Oh, nothing serious. Some lost food. A few startled campers." He proceeded to tell us that we should safeguard our food by hanging it in a tree and that we should never keep food in our tents or in our pockets. And if a bear should come into camp, the ranger told us how to rattle pots and pans to chase it away. He relayed all of this in a quiet, professional voice as he handed me a brochure outlining ways of camping safely in bear country.

On that first trip, we followed all the instructions for avoiding bear problems, and we saw not one bear, not even a hint of a bear. (That's not to say that a bear or two or three hadn't seen us.) I did learn that black bears are as afraid of us as we are of them. But starting with that first trip, we always take precautions. We don't want our names added to the list of campers with "bear problems."

Steve's friend Rick has accompanied us on several of our BWCAW trips. A police officer who worked a tough neighborhood, Rick faced danger every day. But he was reluctant to accompany us when he heard that bears live in the BWCAW. I assured him that in the several years we had been canoeing there, we'd never seen a bear, had one in camp, or seen any evidence of bear damage at our site.

Rick was not convinced. Before our first trip, he quietly asked me if he should bring along his .357 Magnum pistol. "Would that work for bears?"

I suggested he leave his pistol at home, which he did.

That year we camped on Alder Lake for our entire stay, having left behind our lake-to-lake touring and grown accustomed to staying at a base camp, with short day trips. Rick asked about bears in the area, and I told him that we had camped on this lake before and had never seen any evidence of bears. Still, he had a worried look on his face.

Late in the afternoon, after a day of paddling and fishing, Rick was resting in his tent, Steve was fishing from shore, and I was preparing supper, bending over our camp stove, which sat on the fire grate. I had one of my delightful dried noodle meals bubbling in the cooking pot. I looked up and saw, to my considerable surprise, a bear lumbering down the trail from the latrine and heading straight for my bubbling noodles, or so it appeared. I whispered to Steve, and together we watched the bear as it slowly and deliberately made its way into our camp. The animal was huge. I whispered for Rick to look outside the tent. The bear was now about 20 feet away and still headed our direction. Rick unzipped the tent, took one surprised look, and quickly zipped the tent shut again.

The bear stopped when it saw me. We stood staring at each other for what seemed like half an hour (probably a minute or two). Then it ambled off without as much as a grunt or growl.

I told Rick it was safe to come out. He emerged from the tent, looking as white as a sheet. "The bear is gone," I said.

"But will it come back?"

"I don't know," I said. "I doubt it. I think it smelled my fine cooking."

"Yeah, right," said Rick, not at all convinced that we wouldn't have another bear visit.

That evening we cleaned up especially well around camp and hung all our food high in a tree— no stray candy bars in our pockets, no leftover food

To prevent a hungry bear from devouring your food, hang your food bag in a tree—but not too close to the trunk, as bears easily climb trees. Hanging the food bag high also keeps pesky red squirrels away.

of any kind lying about. I suggested that we wash our faces and hands well so we'd have no food smell on them when we went to bed.

The following morning I asked a tired and bedraggled Rick how he had slept. "Not a wink," he said. "That bear was walking around my tent all night."

"I doubt that," I said. "Probably a red squirrel nosing around."

"Sounded like a bear to me."

We had no more bear visits the rest of the week, but Rick was on high alert. I doubt he slept much the entire trip.

The BWCAW does support a considerable population of bears. Minnesota's Department of Natural Resources (DNR) estimates about 20,000 black bears in the state, most of them in the forested area of the northeast. There are only four recorded bear attacks on humans in Minnesota, none of them fatal, but there have been some unfortunate bear encounters. According to Stephen Wilbers in his "Boundary Waters Chronology," in 1987 an emaciated female black bear mauled two campers at Wabang Lake. A nineteen-year-old camper from Tennessee received multiple lacerations and a fractured shoulder bone. The next day, a Minnesota real estate agent on Lake La Croix, a mile from Wabang Lake, met up with a bear and ended up with bites and claw marks on his thigh, forearm, shoulder, head, and neck and a twisted knee. A day later, DNR game wardens shot the bear as it was tearing apart a campsite.

Lynn L. Rogers, noted black bear researcher with the Wildlife Research Institute, wrote, "Unprovoked, predatory attacks by black bears are highly publicized but rare. Such attacks have accounted for all 48 deaths by non-captive black bears across North America this century. Most occurred in Canada and Alaska where the bears had little previous contact with people, rather than in and around established campsites... Deaths from such attacks average a little less than one every two years across the United States and Canada."[1]

Two common and contradictory black bear myths prevail: first, that they are dangerous and relish eating humans; second, that they are cuddly like teddy bears. Both are incorrect, of course.

According to the American Bear Association, black bears are typically shy and easily frightened. They eat mostly berries, nuts, grasses, carrion, and insect larvae. They have color vision and a keen sense of smell and are good tree climbers and swimmers. Black bears (whose color actually ranges from black to cinnamon brown to silver blue and occasionally white) can weigh up to 600 pounds and can run as fast as 35 miles an hour—outrunning one does not appear to be an option.

The American Bear Association has this advice if you should encounter a bear: Stay calm. Do not run. Running may elicit a chase response by the bear. Pick up children so they don't run or scream. Restrain a dog. Don't make eye contact with the bear. Talk in a soothing voice. If the bear stands up, it is not going to attack; it merely wants a better look at you. Back away slowly. If the bear chomps its jaws, lunges, or slaps the ground or brush with a paw, it feels threatened.

Now that you are probably frightened out of your wits at the thought of a black bear encounter, here are some additional safety tips offered by the US Forest Service. You'll note that some of these contradict what the American Bear Association advises, so take your choice.

- Don't store any food in your tent.
- Keep the campsite clean. No spilled grease. Bears are especially attracted to grease. Burn grease in a hot fire, or bury it. And wipe everything clean of grease.
- Wash any food from your face and hands before going to bed.
- Put all food in a waterproof bag and hang it from a tree limb at least 12 feet from the ground and, if possible, 10 feet out from the trunk of a tree.
- If a bear should come into camp, intent on feasting on your week's supply of provisions, yell, bang on pots and pans, wave—generally raise a ruckus to let the critter know it is not welcome.
- Never, ever feed a bear. If you do, you are inviting trouble. They are not cute, harmless creatures. Both their claws and teeth are sharp.

We're always careful to follow these guidelines. And in our more than twenty-five years of camping in the BWCAW, we had a bear in camp just once. It did no damage, except for frightening a police officer out of his wits. Frankly, we've had more problems with red squirrels trying to steal our food.

Wild creatures come in all sizes.

10

Loons and Other Wildlife

Before my first trip to the Boundary Waters, I had never seen nor heard a loon. Now one of the reasons Steve and I return to the BWCAW each year is to see—and especially *hear*—loons. Aldo Leopold wrote, "The Lord did well when he put the loon and his music in the land." For me and for many others, the loons and wilderness go together. Loons can be found in nonwilderness areas, but they seem most comfortable where motorboats and well-groomed lake cottage lawns are missing. Loons spend their summers in the north, which for Minnesota generally means north of Duluth. Starting in October, loons migrate south, where they spend their winters along the Atlantic, Pacific, and Gulf coasts. They return to the north in April and early May.

They are a part of a northern wilderness.

Sigurd T. Olson, Sigurd Olson's son, wrote, "The loon's freedom, independence and simplicity characterize the true spirit of wilderness. Its wild, weird calling does more to create the indescribable feeling of being apart from civilization and being close to the primitive than any other natural phenomenon in the wilderness country."[1]

The common loon (*Gavia immer*) is one of the oldest bird species and is found throughout Canada and the northern tier of states. There are three other loon species: the yellow-billed loon, found in the Far North, usually above the tree line; the red-throated loon, found in Alaska and Canadian Arctic regions; and the arctic loon, native to Alaska and the Hudson Bay region. These are not seen in the BWCAW.[2]

The adult common loon weighs between 8 and 12 pounds, making it larger than a mallard and smaller than a Canada goose. It has a thick neck, a long black bill, and red eyes and is spotty black and white. Because its legs are set far back on its body, it walks awkwardly on land. Males are slightly larger than females, but otherwise the two are identical.

The common loon's calls include a laughlike tremolo; a long and drawn-out wail; a short hoot, used for communication among parents and young; and a yodel, used by male loons to guard their territory.[3]

Loons are not especially shy and thus are easily observed when canoeing in the Boundary Waters. They are terrific swimmers, both above and below the surface. You may see one swimming on the surface, dive, and then emerge many yards away from where you first spotted it. They are good flyers as well, but they need a considerable distance to take off. They remind me of a 747 jet plane lumbering down a runway for a long time before lifting into the air. There is much splashing and wing-pounding before the big bird lifts from a lake's surface and is airborne.

A loon call echoing across a remote lake brings wilderness campers back again and again to the BWCAW.

My Boundary Waters journals contain many entries about loons. I wrote this while we were base camping on Pine Lake.

Wednesday, August 24, 1994. 6:15 AM. Pine Lake
Loons calling this morning at first light. As many times as I've heard the call, I'm always impressed. No other animal or bird call like it. Water is steel gray this morning with a few ripples. Gulls have a rookery a few hundred yards down the shore from our camp. Their raucous, early morning calls are a counterpoint to the loons.

A slight breeze now, blowing out of the southwest. More ripples on the lake, and gurgling sounds as the water sneaks in around the shore rocks. A red squirrel comes down to the lake for a drink. It either doesn't see me or merely ignores me.

A pair of loons approaches from the west, swimming quietly. I now spot more loons straight out from camp a hundred yards or so, making single-note calls, spaced well apart. Seven loons now, in a line, swimming toward our camp. They come as close as maybe 75 yards and the five closest, likely spotting me, all dive at once, disappearing completely with scarcely a ripple remaining on the water's surface. A short time later, they all pop to the surface, one after the other, but now twice as far away.

I have my binoculars in hand, watching the loon antics, listening to their early morning melodies. One of the loons lifts up from the water, calls, flaps its wings, and propels itself forward with loud splashing and continued calling. Soon several more loons are doing this. A loon water game? Their calls echo through the stillness of the morning. And not to be outdone, the gulls commence calling. Loon calls, gull calls—a celebration for the new day, and I'm a part of it.

A lone loon swims but 100 feet from camp, looking me over, inspecting our layout, not participating in the early morning loon games.

One of my most memorable wildlife events in the Boundary Waters involved a bald eagle and an adult and baby loon pair. I wrote this in my journal:

Sunday, July 18, 1999. John Lake
I am sitting on a rock overlooking the lake, reading and occasionally looking up to see a mother loon and her little one swimming a couple hundred yards away. Earlier today I had spotted a mature bald eagle flying over the campsite, its white head and tail reflecting sunlight. I surmised the eagle might have a nest nearby, nothing unusual about that.

112

I hear a loud commotion out on the lake, a loud splashing. I look up to see the eagle and the loon doing battle. The eagle has its eye on the baby loon; the mother loon is not about to let anything happen to her little one. The loon pummels the eagle with its big wings; the eagle tries to do damage with its talons. After a few minutes of pounding and splashing, the eagle lifts from the water and circles overhead, and then a few minutes later dives again at the loon and her offspring. Same result. More splashing and wing pounding. And once more the eagle retreats from the battle to regroup in the sky overhead. This goes on for at least half an hour, the eagle hoping with each dive to snatch up the little loon, the mama loon with each incident successfully warding off the onslaught.

Finally, the eagle gives up. It flies to the top of a tall tree and sits there, humiliated, I'm sure, as eagles are not accustomed to losing a battle. The mother loon and little one go on swimming and fishing and enjoying the day.

In his *Exploring the Boundary Waters,* Daniel Pauly wrote that at least forty species of mammals live in the BWCAW, along with dozens of bird species. Wild animals were a part of my childhood— squirrels, rabbits, fox, weasels (which attacked our chickens from time to time), whitetail deer, hawks, gophers, and more—and I learned at an early age to identify them and appreciate them. But the wildlife in the Boundary Waters is considerably different from that which frequented central Wisconsin in the days of my youth. We saw no bears, moose, wolves, eagles, or loons. Indeed, I'd never seen any of these animals (except in zoos and once in Yellowstone Park) before I started canoeing the Boundary Waters.

We occasionally see a moose in the Boundary Waters. The Minnesota DNR estimates about 7,500 moose in northeastern Minnesota. It's the largest mammal found in the BWCAW, weighing over 1,100 pounds and standing 6 feet at the shoulder. We don't see them every year, and when we do it's a real treat. But like with other wild animals, we keep our distance when we spot one. They can be temperamental, especially a cow with a calf. A mother moose with calf in tow is to be left alone.

In 1992, I noted the following in my journal:

On our way out from Alder Lake, just before the portage to East Bearskin, we spotted a moose feeding in the lake. It was early in the morning, before the sun had come up. When leaving for home, we like an early start, as we have a long drive back to Madison. We packed up at first light and pushed off into the mists and fog that shrouded Alder Lake. I sat in the front, my eyes peeled for stones, snags, and other potential problems, as Steve paddled from the backseat. We moved slowly through the mists as visibility was poor and I surely didn't want to crack into a rock on our way out.

"Rock up ahead," I said to Steve as I spotted what appeared to be a sizable rock thrusting out of the water.

"I see it," Steve said as he continued paddling, changing course a bit to the left to avoid what we were seeing.

I was amazed as the rock began moving—and a moose thrust its head up from the lake's bottom, where it had been feeding.

"Stop paddling," I whispered to Steve. "Do you see what I see?"

We were no more than 20 yards from an enormous bull moose that I guessed might be more than a little upset that we had interrupted his breakfast.

"What do we do now?" Steve asked. He had his paddle ready to reverse course at lightning speed.

"Nothing," I whispered. "Let's just sit tight."

And that's what we did, for what seemed like a long, long time. It probably wasn't but a few minutes. The monster moose—at least, he looked that way as we were so close—slowly emerged from the water, thankfully not in our direction. As he climbed out of the water he grew yet larger and larger—I'd never seen a bigger animal. Once out of the water, the big moose shook himself like a dog might, glanced once in our direction, and disappeared into the woods.

"Well, what did you think of that?" I said, relieved that the moose had other matters on his agenda this day.

"That was something," Steve said. "Really something."

We usually visit the Boundary Waters in late August or early September, when the bug menace is mostly past and the fishing is improving from the dog days of midsummer. Many ducks hatch on Boundary Waters lakes and marshes—another treat for us, as we usually see several duck families. By this time of the season, the little ducks, now mostly grown, are still with their mothers. We usually see them when we are canoeing and often stop and watch. One year something different happened.

We sometimes see moose in the BWCAW, occasionally a big bull.

Thursday, August 26, 1999. Alder Lake

We made camp on the third campsite on the north side of Alder Lake. A nice high place with a breeze. Before our tents were up, a red squirrel came begging. Obviously it had seen our canoe coming, as it had seen others before us. It knew about free lunches. Then a parade of ducks waddled into camp, seven of them, mergansers. Seemed nearly tame. Had they, like the red squirrel, been conditioned to camper handouts?

Before nightfall, the ducks returned several times. Same routine. Same seven, waddling through camp. But one duck was different, much darker than its lighter brown siblings. And an outcast as well, as his nest-mates pecked at him and seemed to push him around. Six ducks wandered away, but the little outcast stayed behind. Steve fed it a piece of bagel, and then another piece. And before you could say "really tame duck," the little dark duck was following Steve all around. Where

Steve went, the little duck followed. All the time we stayed at this campsite, the little duck remained close at hand. Whatever happened to it we'll never know.

The BWCAW lakes provide summer homes to many migratory wild ducks.

An assortment of critters visits our campsites looking for handouts or even attempting robbery. Red squirrels are the cleverest and have stolen more food from us than any bear. As small as they are (about half the size of my fist, with a bushy red tail), red squirrels are both clever and strong. One time, while I was sitting in camp reading and had left the food bag down from its usual spot hanging in a tree, I glimpsed movement out of the corner of my eye. A red squirrel had sneaked into the food bag, plucked out a Snickers, and was scampering off with the big candy bar in its mouth. (It was quite a sight. The Snickers bar was bigger than the squirrel.) But I couldn't let it happen. Stealing food is a cardinal offense in our camp, especially one of our favorite candy bars. I tossed a stick at the sneaky thief, who dropped the candy and rushed up a tree, where it proceeded to scold me loudly. I scolded back: an interspecies confrontation with considerable fury and, I suspect, little understanding. We made sure after that event to keep our food hanging from a tree limb when we weren't preparing a meal.

Occasionally we'll see a field mouse in camp, tan with a lighter belly and big, bulging eyes. Usually they are round and plump, no doubt having spent the summer feasting on crumbs left behind by campers.

Over the years we have spotted lots of beaver sign: beaver houses, beaver dams, evidence of where beavers have cut down trees. And we've seen beavers themselves, on occasion. In a 2006 journal entry I noted the following:

Tuesday, August 22, 2006. John Lake
Late in the afternoon, on our way back to camp from fishing, we spotted the biggest beaver I'd ever seen, swimming near our campsite. Its head, which was all we could see as the rest of the body was underwater, was as large as a good-size dog and even looked a little like a dog. It could swim near as fast as we could paddle. When we got close, the beaver slapped its tail on the water with a report as loud as a gunshot and dove out of sight.

Sometimes we see otters: long and slender, excellent swimmers, and seemingly very inquisitive. In a 1999 journal entry I wrote:

Thursday, August 19, 1999. Alder Lake
I saw a family of otters, five or six of them, when we were fishing yesterday. Wonderful swimmers they are, and they seem to have lots of family fun as well. At one point they swam close to our canoe. Perhaps they are as curious about us as we are about them.

These are but a few of the memorable encounters we've had with Boundary Waters wildlife. Watching these creatures in their environment is always a treat—another reason why we paddle these waters every year.

Good maps are essential in the BWCAW. Knowing how to read one also helps.

11

Where Are We Now?

If you're planning a canoe trip into the Boundary Waters Canoe Area Wilderness, here is my number one piece of advice: Buy a good map. Don't rely on a sketch in the back of some book describing Boundary Waters canoe adventures. Don't try to download one from the Internet. Buy one.

Three companies make the lion's share of BWCAW maps: Fisher, Voyageur, and McKenzie. All three do a good job showing entry points, topography, campsites, and portages on their maps, and all make waterproof maps of the Boundary Waters. The scale of most of these maps is 1½ inches equals a mile. These maps contain stuff you need to know, especially when you're 50 miles from a ranger station, feeling lost (you probably are lost), and you have no one to ask, "Where are we now?"

Some novice BWCAW canoeists make the mistake of buying a map for an area different from where they will be canoeing. Having the wrong map is akin to having a map of Illinois in hand while you are driving in Minnesota—interesting, but not especially useful. The Boundary Waters comprises over a million acres, and there are many, many maps of specific locations available. For instance, to cover the entire BWCAW, Fisher publishes thirty-two maps. I have a desk drawer full of Boundary Waters maps, crinkled and wrinkled and folded incorrectly. I usually pull them all out and reminisce about previous years' trips while planning the next excursion. But map reading has never been one of my talents, although I enjoy looking at them, studying them, and trying (usually without success) to relate what I am seeing in front of me on the ground to a multicolored piece of paper. It may be genetic; I don't know. But I've yet to plan any kind of trip—hiking, driving, or canoeing—when I haven't been lost at least once. Being a man and of German background, being lost is something I seldom admit to, of course.

My first encounter with serious map reading was in army basic training, on maneuvers deep in the "wilds" of Virginia. I was acting sergeant and squad leader of ten mostly novice outdoorsmen and officers in training. We were on a 10-mile march to fight a mock enemy force waiting for us with fake ammunition, extremely loud artillery pieces, and small bags of flour—if one of those hit you, you became a "casualty."

I was in charge of compass and map reading for my squad. The two skills go together, of course. If you don't know what direction you are headed, a map is worthless. Before this exercise, my fellow officer trainees and I had spent long hours in overly warm classrooms listening to the most boring of instructors as he went into great detail about map reading, throwing around terms like *scale*, *topography*, *azimuths*, describing signs and symbols, and discussing the significance of the colors used on maps. He expounded on the nuances of the military lensatic compass, with its protective cover over the dial and wire for sighting in targets and "computing azimuths." Unfortunately, much of what I had heard must have slipped by me on those warm, spring afternoons cooped up in non-air-conditioned classrooms at Fort Eustis, Virginia.

"Are you sure we're going in the right direction?" one of my fellow soldiers asked after we had hiked for a couple of miles in the dark, choosing the path to the right at one fork in the road. "Of course," I said, waving the map I carried with one hand.

We marched on, the sound of artillery fire in the distance. It began raining, and the clay dust turned to red, sticky mud. Finally I could hear small arms fire in a direction different from the one we were headed in. It had to be the battle that we were supposed to be a part of. I quickly suggested a different route, and within a half hour we arrived at the correct open spot in the woods. The battle was over, the flour-dusted casualties counted. The officer in charge, upon seeing me, inquired how many casualties we'd suffered. "None, sir," I said in a loud, clear voice. We were the only casualty-free squad in the entire company and were so recognized. I swore my fellow comrades in arms to silence about the fact that we were lost in the Virginia woods while the battle ensued.

Today when I venture into the BWCAW, I have maps and compass in hand, and I hope that what I see on paper will look something like what appears ahead of me, especially when I'm looking at the location of a campsite or the portage route to the next lake.

In 1986, Steve had just changed jobs and had no vacation time. My youngest son, Jeff, had just completed a summer camp counselor job, so he and I traveled north to Minnesota for a week of canoeing, relaxation, exploring, and a bit of fishing. Like Steve, Jeff had canoed the BWCAW several times, so he suggested we try something different on this trip. "Let's not go to either Ely or Grand Marais," he said.

"So, where?" I asked, having by now developed a certain comfort level with launching our trips from Grand Marais.

"Let's go to Isabella," Jeff said. "There's a ranger station there where we can get permits. And we can put in at Kawishiwi Lake. I've heard it's a good place."

"Okay by me," I said. "What about maps?"

"Should be able to buy one in Isabella," Jeff said.

We left Madison at 5:30 AM. This time I was driving a 1984 Nissan pickup truck with a topper and a canoe rack. As on previous trips, at Duluth we turned onto Highway 61 and drove along Lake Superior until we arrived at the intersection with Highway 1, a few miles north of Silver Bay. On Highway 1 we traveled through thick forestland, across little marshes and streams, and then up and down hills with no views of the blue waters of Lake Superior that we had left behind. We drove through Finland, where a sign said, Isabella, 16 miles.

Isabella is prominently marked on the Minnesota road map, and I expected a fair-size town. What we found was a tavern, a general store, a gas station, a few houses, a church, and the ranger station.

Later I learned that Isabella had been a logging town that came into existence in about 1906. Its little post office opened in 1912. Isabella is about halfway between Ely, to the northwest, and Silver Bay, to the southeast, sitting all by its isolated self perched on the highest point in Minnesota, 2,000 feet, its apparent sole claim to fame.

We stopped at the general store and inquired about fishing licenses and BWCAW maps. A polite store clerk said, "Oh, we don't sell fishing licenses, nor does anybody else here in Isabella. Closest town for fishing licenses is Finland. I don't know about canoe maps. You could probably get one at the ranger station. Don't get any call for that sort of thing here."

We turned the pickup around and headed back toward Finland, where we bought fishing licenses and asked about BWCAW maps. "You can probably get a map at the ranger station in Isabella," the fellow at the Finland gas station said. "Good luck with the fishing."

Once more back in Isabella, we pulled into the parking lot at the ranger station. "Nope, we don't sell any maps here. All we got are BWCAW permits," the ranger on duty said when I inquired. "Got a map you can look at, though. Here's a piece of paper if you want to make some notes."

For the next several minutes I copied down names of lakes, rivers, lengths of portages, and campsite locations in the area we wanted to canoe. I sketched the most primitive of maps—as it turned out, not a very accurate one.

With permit and "map" in hand, we piled into the Nissan and followed a dusty, twisty dirt road for

Often what you see in front of you bears little resemblance to a map, especially on foggy days.

30 miles until we finally arrived at Kawishiwi Lake. There we found a five-place campsite, where we parked the pickup. Our permit started the next day, so we slept in the back of the pickup, which turned out to be quite comfortable with air mattresses and sleeping bags. Any qualms I had about our lack of an adequate map moved to the back of my mind as I dreamed about big fish, beautiful vistas, and loon calls echoing in the night.

By 8:30 the next morning, we pushed off, Jeff paddling in the back of the canoe and me in the front with my hand-drawn map in a plastic bag and my compass at the ready. I paddled when I wasn't map-looking or compass-checking. Jeff listened to my instructions and steered us in the direction I pointed my canoe paddle. The lake was smooth, not a ripple. The paddling was easy. Life was good.

We paddled from Kawishiwi Lake into the Kawishiwi River and then into Square Lake. The map was perfect—so what that we had no idea about distances, except for the portages for which I had jotted down lengths. Canoeing should be an adventure! The voyageurs who canoed these lakes long before we recreational canoeists came along surely didn't have fancy maps. They made do. We were making do.

It was a 20-rod portage to another river and to Kawasachong Lake—a mouthful of a lake, but it appeared on my handmade map. We had a little trouble finding the portage to Townline Lake, but we were in no hurry. The sun was bright, the water blue, and a loon flew over calling its mysterious call. When the portage wasn't where it was supposed to be according to my map and I had no idea where to find it, I said to Jeff, "Remember, it's the journey and not the destination that's important."

"But where's the damn portage?" said Jeff, not impressed with my attempt at travel philosophy.

We paddled on, crowding close to shore so we wouldn't miss any telltale signs of where a canoe had left a scuff mark on rocks or underbrush seemed trampled. After a half hour of paddling we finally found it. From there we portaged 181 rather grueling rods to little Townline Lake and then quite easily found the 91-rod portage to Lake Polly, where we had planned to spend the night. We even found a campsite without difficulty; my hand-drawn map indicated right where it should be.

"Who says you can't canoe in the Boundary Waters without a fancy map?" I said.

"It's only the first day, Dad. And besides, we've already been lost once."

"Not lost, Jeff. It was the portage that was lost."

"Right," Jeff said as he unloaded the canoe and began setting up our tent while I organized the cooking site.

"Beautiful lake," Jeff remarked after we'd finished setting up camp, pulled our Grumman canoe out of the lake, and sat relaxing on the huge, flat stones that fronted our campsite. The temperature was in the seventies, and a light breeze blew from the southwest, just enough to create a light chop on the water. Little waves politely nudged the rocks, creating a gentle, melodious sound.

After an hour or so of fishing, never out of sight of our camp, and with no fish to show for our efforts, we ate dinner, cleaned up camp, and watched the sunset with loon calls in the background. I saw horsetail clouds building in the west, a sign of rain to come.

During the night, I awakened to the rumble of thunder, a flash of lightning, and the sound of raindrops on the tent roof. The rain continued through breakfast as we sat under our rain fly, savoring second cups of coffee and gazing out at rain-enshrouded Lake Polly. Then a breeze came up from the west, the sun burned through the clouds, and our dreary spirits soared.

"Good fishing day," I said.

"But how about a better lake, maybe one with fish in it," said Jeff.

I had scratched Koma Lake on my hurriedly made map, but I had not indicated the location of the portage from Lake Polly.

"It's gotta be on the north end of the lake," Jeff said. "Shouldn't be a problem to find it."

What my handmade map failed to disclose were the several little fingers and bays on the north end of the lake. The portage was likely at the end of one of these bays, but which one? We tried the first one. Nothing. We turned around and canoed back to try the second bay, which was longer and had a big bend in it.

As we rounded the bend, much to our surprise, we came upon four young women sunbathing on a big rock outcropping. When they spotted us, all four jumped to their feet and stood in a row, facing us. The two at the ends held up a huge towel that came nearly up to the necks of the four of them. We waved and smiled. They waved and smiled.

"Looks like we interrupted a little nude sun-bathing," Jeff said, grinning from ear to ear.

"Appears so," I said. "Keep paddling. Make it look like we know where we're going."

We paddled on, not at all confident that we were on the correct route to the portage. The women clearly thought they had chosen a place to sunbathe with no canoe traffic—they surely didn't expect to see a couple of lost canoeists paddling by. We paddled to the end of the second bay. No sign of a portage.

We once more turned the canoe around and paddled back the way we had come, this time a little farther from shore. The young women jumped to their feet again. This time they were not smiling.

"Hand me the binoculars," Jeff asked. "I want to make sure they were doing what we thought they were doing."

I handed him the binoculars.

"Well?" I said after a minute or two.

"They were," said Jeff, smiling as he handed back the binoculars.

We paddled on and half an hour later found the portage to Lake Koma.

"There are some benefits to not having a decent map," Jeff said that evening as we laughed about the afternoon's misadventures. We hadn't caught any fish in Lake Koma either, after all the bother to find the place.

Even with decent maps, I have succeeded in helping us become thoroughly lost. Ten years after the nudist incident, we once again became slightly confused about where we were. Steve was with me this time.

Wednesday, August 28, 1996. 3:30 P.M. Duncan Lake

Map-reading problem yesterday. Our goal was to portage from Duncan Lake to Partridge Lake, where we planned some fishing. Without realizing it, we portaged to Moss Lake—we thought we were on Partridge. When we portaged out of what we thought was Partridge and back to Duncan, we stumbled through the woods and ended up on a road. There should not be a road, according to my map.

Fellow in a pickup came by. We flagged him down. "Any chance you could tell us where we are?" I asked sheepishly.

"Yup, you're on the road to Hungry Jack Lake."

"Thank you," I said. Steve and I studied the map once more and decided we had made only a 180-degree error—best I fess up, I had made a 180-degree error. After more portaging and a lot more paddling, we finally arrived back on Duncan and found our campsite.

These are the most memorable of the many times I have pored over our maps and wondered, "Where in the heck are we, anyway?" For us it's all part of our BWCAW experience.

12

Family Adventure

In 1988 our canoe party included Steve and me, my youngest son, Jeff, daughter Sue, and her husband, Wayne—all in their twenties, except for me. I was fifty-four at the time. Sue was a first grade teacher, Steve a newspaper photographer, and Jeff just completing two years as a master counselor for an alternative youth camp in North Carolina—a wilderness camp where first-offender boys were sent in lieu of going to prison. For two years he had been camping full-time with ten not-to-be trusted boys who were as likely to steal his wallet as help with camp chores. Jeff was burned out and looking for a career alternative.

My three kids had canoed the BWCAW several times, but for my son-in-law, Wayne, this was the first time. Our equipment included two 17-foot Grumman canoes, and two Eureka tents—one four-person tent for the boys and me and a two-person tent for Sue and Wayne. I drove my Nissan pickup; Jeff drove his Ford Ranger.

We picked up BWCAW permits and bought fishing licenses in Grand Marais and then drove the 50-plus miles of the Gunflint Trail to the Trails End Campground, where we spent the night. Early on

Tuesday morning we put in at Round Lake, portaged 142 rods to Missing Link Lake, and paddled across Missing Link Lake to face an arduous 366-rod portage to Tuscarora Lake, our first day's destination. The weather was hot, temperatures in the low nineties, the mosquitoes hungry, and the portages difficult. But we were fresh, my crew was young, and I heard little complaining. On the portages, Steve and Jeff carried the canoes and light packs; the three remaining carried the heavier packs. We discovered that humor takes a different form under difficult conditions. My daughter, Sue, about five feet two, thin and trim, carried a huge backpack on the long portage from Missing Link to Tuscarora—it must have weighed 50 pounds. It took both Wayne and Steve to help her put it on and adjust it. She plodded ahead of me on the crooked trail strewn with rocks. When the path wasn't climbing steeply it was falling away quickly. Sue, Wayne, and I walked under the weight of our packs with our heads down and our bodies leaning forward.

I heard a gasp from Sue and looked up to see her flying through the air in a complete somersault, heavy pack still in place. She landed on the pack, laughing at her misfortune. She had caught one of her hiking boots under a root, which completely upended her. She was uninjured, except for her pride, and we all chuckled about the incident around the campfire that evening.

The long portage to Tuscarora was worth it. I had done a little research on the lake and learned that it was 2 miles across, 800 acres of open water, and at places 120 feet deep. I had also discovered

Carrying a heavy pack, daughter Susan takes a tumble while portaging. No injuries, but she is embarrassed.

that the west side of the lake boasts some of the oldest forest in the entire region, some of the trees more than two hundred years old. The lake supposedly has a substantial population of lake trout—one of the features that attracted me, because I had never caught a lake trout in my many years of fishing.

Tuscarora has ten campsites scattered around its several miles of shore, one of them on an island, and essentially none of the campsites are visible from each other. We put up our tents at a campsite on an outcropping jutting into the lake and with a glorious view to the south.

On one side of the lake we found huge stone cliffs rising straight up from the water's edge, a perfect place for diving after we determined that the water was many feet deep at the edge of the cliff. I was content to watch as those younger than I leaped into space and dove beneath the cool blue waters on this unusually hot summer day in the north.

No lake trout found our variety of baits attractive, so fishing proved a bust, but sometimes one must allow beauty to trump more practical endeavors. The place was indeed beautiful and our campsite one of the best we'd ever had in the several years we'd been in the BWCAW.

Around the campfire at night we played cards, told stories, and succeeded in scaring the bejeebers out of son-in-law Wayne, who confessed, "I've never been in a place where it gets so dark or is so quiet." His brothers-in-law stretched the truth more than a little as they told about bear attacks in the night and unpredicted storms that tear down tents and soak occupants. (As it turned out, the latter proved more truth than fiction.)

On Thursday morning we packed up and portaged 366 rods back to Missing Link Lake. As Jeff said, when we finally arrived on Missing Link, "That portage was as miserable the second time as it was the first."

Missing Link Lake is small, only 41 acres, with three campsites. The temperature was still in the low nineties as we set up camp, and clouds were building in the west, a sure sign of a storm to come. The storm's first wave hit about 6:00 PM, after we'd finished eating and were cleaning up. Loud thunder, jagged flashing lightning, small hail driven on a potentially dangerous wind, and rain that fell horizontally in sheets. With the rain-softened ground and the strong winds, the tent pegs for my rain fly pulled loose and some of my gear got soaked. Storm after storm pounded us through the night, the thunder rolling across the lake. Lightning illuminated the inside of the tent for an instant; the next moment it was as dark as the inside of a cave.

The morning dawned clear as five somewhat-wet campers emerged from their tents to face the day. We packed up our wet equipment for a 142-rod portage and a modest paddle before we found our trucks and were on our way home.

I learn much about my grown children on these trips: their love for the outdoors, their willingness to put up with less than pleasant conditions, their concern about each other's careers and job choices. Much talk that week took place between Jeff and his siblings. In September Jeff quit his job in North Carolina and moved to Vail, Colorado, with an entirely different future in front of him. This career move was discussed among siblings in a place where everyone had time to think, contemplate, and consider.

The Boundary Waters canoe camping experience means different things to different people—and different things to the same people at different times in their lives. This is a place where you can come out from behind yourself and have a serious look around. I know I've done that at times in the Boundary Waters. My children have, too.

Fishing from a canoe is always fun. Here we hook a small northern pike, which we will release.

13

Fish Stories

I've been a subscriber to the *Boundary Waters Journal* for many years, and I can't recall a single issue that didn't have one or more fish stories: tales of some monster northern pike that someone brought up out of the depths, an enormous walleye caught with some exotic lure, or, more likely, a dinner-plate-size small-mouth bass. First-person stories of fishing escapades fill the pages of the *BWJ* and do, I must say, make for interesting reading, as Steve and I enjoy fishing (and reading about fishing) as much as the next canoeist.

For some of us, fishing seems a part of our DNA, going back to ancestors who fished not so much for the fun of it, but out of necessity. During the Depression years and World War II, when I was a kid, the fish we caught, especially in winter, contributed greatly to our food supply.

But unlike some Boundary Waters visitors, we do not depend on fish as a food source, though we did in the early days. Now we are content to catch and release; and we don't spend a lot of time fishing—a few hours in the morning, a few more before sunset. For us, fishing is a pleasant and relaxing aside to our canoe country visit. If we catch fish, wonderful. If we don't, that's wonderful, too. My father, a great fisherman who loved the sport and fished often, said, "Fishing is always good. Catching is sometimes not so good."

Over the years I've collected an assortment of fishing rods, lures, and other "essential" fishing equipment. (Essential is, of course, in the eye of the beholder. Essential for me often evokes a "What are you going to do with that?" response from my wife.) For fishing in the Boundary Waters, we select gear that is absolutely necessary and no more. After all, we have to carry it along with everything else. These days I bring along two spinning rods, both collapsible. They are 5½ feet long when extended, no more than 10 inches or so when collapsed. I also bring two spinning reels, with 10-pound test monofilament line on each.

I depend on jointed Rapala lures, the kind that are 3 inches long or so, look very much like a minnow when in the water, and float. (I once used lures that sink and was constantly getting hooked onto something that wasn't a fish. I left too many of these lures on the bottom of BWCAW lakes.) I bring several Rapala lures, some black on top and white on the bottom, some blue on top, others red on top. On different days, fish seem to prefer different colors. I say "seem to" because I have no idea why fish will strike at my lure on Tuesday and ignore everything I throw at them on Wednesday.

I bring along some extra brass swivels (used to attach the line to the lures), pliers to remove hooks (I use a Leatherman, which includes a knife, pliers, and more, which I carry on my belt), and a small measuring tape. Estimates of fish length are notoriously inaccurate, and you can't brag about a fish that you haven't measured. Once you've measured the fish and know precisely its length, it's okay to add a couple inches when you tell the story. Fish stories are much more believable when you begin with "This fish measured." (Sorry, fishermen, I've likely just divulged a time-honored secret.) If you forget your measuring device, an old trick I learned many years ago is to measure with a dollar bill, which is exactly 6 inches long.

I keep my lures and other small fishing equipment in a little fishing box that I can carry in my pocket when we portage. Steve has essentially the same fishing equipment as I do, except that he prefers an open-faced spinning rod.

In the early years I always carried a net, thinking I would need one when I hooked one of those 40-inch northerns. Two things happened over the years. On portages the net caught on brush and other assorted protrusions along the trail, making the portage more challenging than it already was. And we never came close to hooking a 40-inch northern; indeed, we'd be thrilled to catch one half that size. Everything we've caught in recent years we've been able to bring into the canoe sans net.

In recent years Steve and I have a fishing wager that involves who will buy breakfast at the Blue Water Café in Grand Marais when we come out the last morning of canoeing. We've refined the wager a bit so that in 2009 it had the following stipulations: First fish caught over 6 inches buys the other guy one-half breakfast. Largest fish caught during the week buys one-half breakfast.

Tuesday, September 1, 2009. Bearskin Lake

We fished along the north shore of Bearskin Lake this afternoon, moving slowly and enjoying the beautiful late-summer day. Within a half hour I hooked about an 8-inch smallmouth bass, and after a little discussion about the fish's size, was assured of at least one-half free breakfast as it was the first fish caught. A few minutes later, Steve caught first a 4-inch smallmouth and then a 5-incher (we had found our measuring stick). So far, with my 8-inch fish, I was in line for an entire breakfast. Steve was getting grumpy, because he was the one who had come up with the new stipulations for this year's fishing wager.

Wednesday, September 2, 2009. Bearskin Lake

Within an hour I caught two more smallmouth bass, one 10 inches and one 12 inches. Steve was becoming desperate. He checked the lure I was using and began using a similar one. He observed where I was tossing my lure and he tried similar places. "I've got one," he finally announced. "Not doing much fighting, though."

When he pulled the fish from the water, a look of total defeat spread across his face. "This little perch is not as long as my lure."

As it turned out, we caught no more fish on that trip, and a few mornings later I feasted on flapjacks, two eggs over-easy, and several tasty strips of bacon. And Steve paid.

In our early years in the BWCAW, two or three of our meals featured fresh-caught fish.

Wednesday, July 18, 1990. John Lake
We paddled the length of John Lake and then portaged to Pike Lake, where we spent the afternoon fishing. We caught eight good-size smallmouth bass, one we estimated to weigh at least 3 pounds. What a fight it put up, especially for fisherman working from a canoe where quick movements are a no-no. Fish for supper, with macaroni and cheese—a rather strange combination, but when you're hungry, complaining slides into the background.

Over the years we've hooked many smallmouth bass, a few good-size ones, and all pole-benders.

Sometime in the mid-1990s, we moved from catching and eating to catching and releasing. I'm trying to remember exactly why. Best I can recall is the practical reason of having fish on our camp menu and then not catching any. Some years we caught not one fish. I'm sure the BWCAW promotional people don't like to hear that, but at least for us it's true. I don't want to offer excuses—oh, believe me, I've got a pocket full of them—but our problem is we've never taken fishing seriously enough. I suspect a serious fisherman will catch fish every year—or not?

Wednesday, August 27, 1997. Alder Lake
Not 50 feet from shore I caught a 14-inch smallmouth bass. Largest smallmouth I've caught in awhile. We released it after measuring and photographing it.

Thursday, August 19, 1999. Alder Lake
Fishing has been excellent this year. We've already caught sixteen smallmouth bass ranging from 7 to 16 inches. Steve caught the big 16-incher last night. Nice fish. Fought like everything. This may be our record year for most fish caught since we've been coming here. We released all of them.

Thursday, September 4, 2003. John Lake
Sun peeking above the treetops to the east at 7:00 AM. A welcome sight after yesterday, which was a cloudy, cold, windy, character-building, downright ornery day. A day of promise ahead—and questions. Will the temperature climb into the 60s? Will the fish bite?

Climbed into the canoe about 10:00 and paddled toward the west end of the lake in search of a little stream

Not of bragging size, this northern pike was still a handful on light spinning gear.

that snakes through a marshy area and then connects to another little, very secluded lake. Soon after arriving in the little lake, a big smallmouth bass hit my lure, leaped into the air, and broke my line. Steve hooked, and we brought into the canoe a 15-inch northern pike. But that's it. That's all we caught. A great day for paddling. But little bragging about the fishing.

I've been a fisherman since I was four years old and my dad took me ice fishing. I've never gotten over the thrill of landing a fish, whether it was pulling a bluegill through a hole chopped in the ice, bringing in a perch with a long cane pole, or reeling in a smallmouth bass with lightweight spinning rods. The anticipation of what might be lurking in the depths, considering my bait, and the thrill of a fish fighting at the end of my line have never waned. So I continue to fish, because it brings me together with friends and relatives and offers one more "excuse" for enjoying the outdoors. It's easier to say I've been fishing than to fess up that I was really just enjoying the day. If I catch a fish, it is clearly a bonus.

Base camping—staying in one place and making day-trips—is how we wilderness camp these days.

14

Base Camping

After several years of loop camping, trying to see how many Boundary Waters lakes we could canoe in a week, Steve and I changed our tactic. We began base camping—selecting one campsite and staying there, venturing off to canoe and explore other lakes during the day, but returning to our base site every evening. We find it to be a more relaxing and less strenuous way of enjoying the Boundary Waters.

Some might say we're too lazy to take down and put back together a campsite every day. Some might say we're just avoiding the possibility of not finding a campsite at the end of a hard day of paddling during busy canoe season, when the competition for camp-sites is at its peak. It's true that once or twice we had difficulty finding an open campsite and had to paddle an extra hour or two into the evening when we would rather have been enjoying the sunset and a second cup of coffee.

The most important reason we base camp is because we find it more relaxing, peaceful, and more in line with how we want to enjoy the Boundary Waters. Perhaps as much as anything, we don't want to hurry at anything anymore, whether it's putting up a tent, fixing supper, or paddling across a lake. We want to move as slowly as is comfortable, with no one saying, "We'd better pack up and get going if we're gonna make X Lake this evening."

With base camping, we have many choices: Stay the day in camp and read, nap, sit by the water's edge, listen to the campfire snap and crackle, write in a journal, begin the great American novel, craft a poem. Putter around camp—cut a little wood, fuss a little more with the meals, sharpen a hunting knife, fiddle with a new compass.

Or, we can hop in the canoe and go fishing on the base camp lake or, with a modest portage, on a nearby lake. We do a lot of exploring, looking for places where others seldom go. Nearly every lake has interesting nooks and crannies, little bays and inlets, streams that run into and out of them. We usually take our fishing rods along, just in case, but we sometimes find it as interesting to look for wild-flowers, beaver houses, wild rice patches, a wasp nest hanging on a low tree branch, a wild animal. One time we came upon a female moose dozing on shore, not especially put off by our presence—she didn't even get up. She continued chewing her cud and flicking her ears at a menacing fly. Oftentimes, especially when we canoe up a narrow stream with little evidence that others have been there before us, we have the feeling that we are going back in time and have left the world behind us. The only sounds are those of the paddles and the canoe sliding through the water, easing our way back into history.

With many years of loop camping under our belts, we have seen many lakes, too many portages, and a goodly number of campsites. In my journal I have noted details about campsites including view, mosquito potential, ease for docking the canoe, distance from other campsites (usually not a problem, but once we did experience a too-loud party at a campsite across the lake from us), and an ample area for rock sitting and reading with the preferred southerly or westerly view. As we've gotten older, both Steve and I enjoy solitude when we're canoeing, meaning we'd rather not see other canoeists. It's not that we're antisocial—we both have jobs where we meet lots of people—but when we canoe we want wilderness, not people. We prefer the sounds of nature over the sounds of partying.

For several years we base camped on Pine Lake in the eastern region of the Boundary Waters, with access from the Arrowhead Trail. Pine Lake is easily reached by a civilized paddle across McFarland Lake, which is outside the BWCAW. Entry 68 is a short portage or a fairly easy paddle in a short, rocky stream that connects Pine and McFarland lakes. Pine Lake has about ten campsites, but it is a big lake, about 8 miles long, so they are scattered well apart. We have camped at several sites along the north shore and at the rocky point on the east shore, not far from the portage.

Base camping at Pine Lake gave us access to several nearby lakes, where we regularly fished. Getting to Long Lake and Stump Lake required a 140-rod portage from Pine, little Gadwall Lake was but 80 rods, and even smaller Vale Lake was 63 rods away. And of course the portages, with only the canoe, our lunch packs, and fishing equipment to carry, were

While base camping we explore the nooks and crannies of the lakes in the area of our camp.

many times easier than hauling all of our camping equipment with us.

Pine Lake itself is an excellent fishing lake, with walleye, smallmouth bass, and northern pike—we've caught all three species plus now and again a perch or two. But beyond fishing, Pine Lake has enormous natural beauty with its steep hills, rocky shores, and trees, especially white cedar trees that come down to the water's edge.

We have also enjoyed canoeing to the far west end of Pine Lake and then hiking the short distance to Johnson Falls, deep within the woods and undisturbed by any development.

Thursday, July 18, 1991. Pine Lake

We parked our canoe at the end of Pine Lake and followed a crooked, rough, muddy, stony, often steep trail to 25-foot Johnson Falls, deep in the woods. It's the most primitive waterfall I've ever seen—and simply not easy to get to. We lingered at the falls for some time, listening to the water tumble over the rocks and watching the spray fly into the air. What a peaceful place it is.

After our first sweaty and mosquito-laden trip to the falls, Steve, with his cynical sense of humor, said, "I expected to see a busload of tourists at the top of the falls, taking pictures, smashing down the vegetation, and talking loud about the wilderness. I suspected there was an easier approach to the falls on the other side." There isn't an easier approach. Getting there is hard work, especially on a warm day when the mosquito squadrons are out in force. We were the only tourists that day.

After several bad experiences with the wind on Pine Lake, including dumping our canoe, we abandoned Pine Lake for calmer waters. For the last few years we have base camped on John Lake, which is smaller and much less susceptible to wind and waves. John Lake is only about a mile and half long and a quarter mile or so wide and has only three campsites, each of which is quite suitable for base camping.

To get to John Lake, we put in at the boat landing on Little John Lake, across the road from the McFarland Lake landing. A short paddle across Little John, which is outside the BWCAW, brings us to entry point 69 and an interesting but little creek that connects Little John to John Lake. Most of the time, especially when the water is at normal levels, the rapids are easy to manage, even with a loaded canoe. But one year it was impossible. Beavers had built a dam across the short stream, and we had to portage from Little John—not too difficult, but an annoyance when we expected we could paddle right on through.

John Lake may not be as rich a fishing lake as others, but we've caught our share of good-size smallmouth bass and even a respectable northern pike or two. Like nearly every other lake in the Boundary Waters, it has interesting areas to explore. On the east end of John Lake is the Royal River, which requires a 60-rod portage to reach canoeable water and a fascinating paddle to little Royal Lake. And if you are really in an exploring mood, a 120-rod portage will take you to North Fowl Lake and the Canadian border.

A 180-rod portage on the other end of John Lake takes you to East Pike Lake, a long, narrow, fairly shallow lake. Just before the portage on the right is a small, navigable stream that Steve and I have explored several times. It winds its way through reeds and pond lilies until it reaches a small unnamed pond, where we have caught some nice-size smallmouth bass, have found beaver activity, and often see wild ducks. It's a quiet, peaceful little side journey.

We've changed our camping strategy a little from the days when we visited a new campsite each day. Now we are more deliberate about the campsite we select. We spend a little more time setting up our tents, making them as weather resistant as possible, which means making sure all the tent pegs are firmly in place, and selecting a site where the ground is level, which helps sleeping.

We also, I must confess, bring along a little more equipment than when we fussed about keeping everything light for easier portaging. Now we each have a folding chair, and I even bring along a small folding table with a little slot for my coffee cup, which I keep at the ready when I'm writing.

We have no complaints against those who wish to travel from day to day and see new lakes, find new campsites, and enjoy the Boundary Waters in this fashion. After all, that's what we did for several years. But at this stage in our lives, base camping is right for us, allowing us to enjoy what we want to experience in this special place with its clear lakes, deep woods, and immense quiet.

Backwater areas evoke a sense of mystery, as we often discover interesting little ponds that sometimes provide great fishing but always provide another view of wilderness.

15

Day-Tripping

In fall 2008 Steve injured his back and was incapacitated for several months. Nonetheless, in April 2009 I submitted an application for a permit to camp in the Boundary Waters. With a permit for early September, we both hoped that Steve would recover enough for our annual trip. He had surgery on his back in early July, and the doctor warned him to do no heavy lifting, no twisting, and to avoid bending over for six to nine months. Canoe camping is not terribly difficult, but it isn't easy, either. There is a canoe to carry, backpacks to handle, paddling to do, portages to traverse. I am in reasonably good shape and could do my share but certainly not all the work required. And as my friends remind me, I'm not as young as I once was.

By late July it was clear that Steve's proper recovery meant not doing most of these things—paddling was okay, but we would have to launch the canoe. And there would be no backpack lugging or canoe carrying for Steve. We agreed it was a year for Steve to recover. I canceled our reservation and for the first time in more than twenty-five years prepared to miss a year canoe camping.

But we soon discovered an alternative, a way to experience the Boundary Waters—much of it, anyway—without the heavy lifting. We became a part of the day-tripper group. A day-tripper canoes in the Boundary Waters from early morning to late afternoon but does not spend the night there in a tent. Although a reservation is not required, day-trippers must fill out a BWCAW Visitor's Self-issued Permit and have the permit in possession while in the Boundary Waters. The permit is free, and permit boxes are located at entry points. (From October 1 through April 30, these permits are also used for overnight camping in the BWCAW.)

I turned to the Internet and looked for a place adjacent to the Boundary Waters that we could use as a base camp. I found more than twenty resorts, cabin rentals, and assorted outfitters scattered along the Gunflint Trail. There are others, of course, in other locations. With a little digging I learned that several of the resorts go back to the early 1920s and 1930s—Hungry Jack Lodge, Bearskin Lodge, Old Northwoods Lodge, and Nor'western Lodge are examples. Other lodges along the Gunflint Trail include Tuscarora, Seagull, Trout Lake, Windigo, Way of the Wilderness, Loon Lake, Gunflint, and Clearwater.

Steve and I selected Hungry Jack Lodge as our jumping-off place, one of the oldest resorts on the Gunflint Trail. Hungry Jack Lodge is on Hungry Jack Lake, some 30 miles from Grand Marais. As the story goes, Hungry Jack Lake was named in 1884, when US government surveyors were mapping the land and naming the many lakes they encountered. Andrew Jackson (Jack) Scott, a well-known trapper,

Hungry Jack Lodge opened in 1924 and is one of the oldest lodges on the Gunflint Trail.

hunter, and guide, worked as a guide for the surveyors. The survey crew reached what is now Hungry Jack Lake in late fall. They decided to camp there until spring, but they were low on supplies, so the surveyors strapped on snowshoes and set off for Grand Marais to replenish their food supply, leaving Jack Scott at the makeshift camp. While they were gone, a huge snowstorm struck the area, and the surveyors were delayed in returning. When they finally returned, Jack Scott was starving. As the story goes, one surveyor called out, "Are you hungry, Jack?" His reply: "I am a hungry Jack, I'm about starved to death!"

By 1923 the Gunflint Trail had been extended from Grand Marais to Hungry Jack Lake, primarily to assist in forest-fire prevention. Jesse Gapen built a lodge—really a rustic log cabin—on the lake in

1924. In 1931 the log lodge burned, and though the country was in the midst of the Great Depression, Gapen rebuilt with logs harvested near the lake. The new lodge was 126 feet long and 84 feet wide, one of the largest log buildings in the Midwest. The lodge and resort was sold to the Patrick McDonald family in 1958, and they operated it for fourteen years.

In 1972 Jerry Parson bought the property. The cabins were in poor shape and required considerable renovation. In December of that year, fire claimed the big log lodge. Parson, not one to give up, bought a former DNR log building in Grand Marais, took it apart log by log, and moved it to Hungry Jack Lake. The new lodge was open for business by the end of 1973.

Forrest Parson owns the Hungry Jack Lodge on Hungry Jack Lake, an entryway to the BWCAW.

Jerry Parson and his son, Forrest Parson, a 2003 graduate of University of Wisconsin–Stout's program in hotel, restaurant, and tourism management, operated the resort until Jerry Parson's death on December 25, 2006. Forrest Parson continues to operate the lodge and resort. In March 2008 fire once more destroyed the lodge, but Parson quickly decided to rebuild.

Today Hungry Jack Lodge resort has fourteen cabins and fourteen campsites, plus a new log lodge. It is the only resort on Hungry Jack Lake. In September 2009 I talked to Parson, then twenty-nine years old, about his goals for the lodge and resort. By then the new log lodge was nearly completed. "I want to go back to how we did it before, but with the option to do ten times more. I work hard because I want to succeed," he told me. Forrest Parson represents a new generation of resort owners who are savvy to changing customer interests and knowledgeable about alternative approaches to marketing, including expanded use of the Internet. Parson told me that the resort has had guests from every state plus twenty-seven countries, which says something about the reputation of the resort and the draw of the Boundary Waters Canoe Area Wilderness.

Steve and I easily found the portage from Hungry Jack into Bearskin Lake on our first day there, an easy 20-plus-rod portage. With Steve's carrying restrictions, we portaged our Kevlar canoe, with me carrying one end and Steve the other. A day pack with our lunches, fishing equipment, and rain gear was all we toted in with us. From Bearskin, you can portage 60 rods into Daniels Lake or 75 rods into

Duncan Lake. An 80-rod portage from Duncan Lake and you're in Rose Lake, at the Canadian border.

As an alternative for those with health or mobility challenges, day-tripping in the BWCAW and staying at an adjacent resort makes sense. It especially made sense to Steve and me in 2009, as we would have broken our long string of yearly trips into the land of the loon had we not chosen a resort as our base of operations.

With thousands of baby boomers reaching retirement age, and more to come, day-tripping is one way for this older generation to enjoy much of the Boundary Waters canoe experience without the physical requirement of tent camping. Along with the older baby boomers are thousands of people with health and physical challenges who also can enjoy a wilderness experience. No tents, sleeping bags, heavy food packs, camp stoves, or tarps are necessary—just a canoe, paddles, and perhaps a light day pack to carry rain gear, maps, and lunch. Portaging is obviously much simpler and considerably less strenuous without the heavy portage packs to carry.

When Steve and I decided to day camp in 2009, I was a bit leery about telling my friends. I could hear them saying, "To experience the Boundary Waters, you've got to sleep in a tent and sit by a campfire." No question about it, tent camping in the Boundary Waters is a powerful, satisfying, and enjoyable experience. But for those who for whatever reason can't or don't want to tent camp, day-tripping is a reasonable alternative. It's a different experience from tent camping to be sure, but with day-tripping you can fish, explore nooks and crannies and hidden lake bays, listen to loon calls, and experience the quiet of a place where people are few, motors are nonexistent, and solitude is a possibility.

So for those tent campers who believe that their way is the only way to truly explore the Boundary Waters, I say…well, I don't say it. I smile and think, *Wait until for one reason or another you can't tent camp anymore.* Will you stay away from the BWCAW in the interest of having a "pure" experience or none at all? My guess is that the Boundary Waters, like a magnet, will draw you there and will welcome you no matter what your medical challenges or physical limitations, as it has welcomed Steve and me.

Beyond the moose, deer, loons, and bears, don't forget to stop and view the little creatures. A big green frog deserves a little attention.

Part III: Challenges

For those who have learned to hear its song,
the earth can sooth the troubled heart, refresh the weary,
soften the hardened, redirect the lost.

—Steve Van Metre, *The Earth Speaks*

16

Thunderstorms

In the quiet of the Boundary Waters, when a storm begins building in the southwest, the first thunder comes as a low growl, almost imperceptible, but there's no mistaking the sound. As dark clouds build and the sun disappears, the growling thunder becomes louder, now more rumble than growl. The sky grows darker and lightning flashes, cutting through the darkness, followed by thunder, louder with each flash. It is nature's theater in the round, especially when we are in camp, looking out across the expanse of a lake, lightning flashing in the distance and thunder rolling across the water, echoing, filling the vast space of silence with primitive sound. In evening the show is even more spectacular, competing with the most elaborate Fourth of July fireworks.

The storm clouds churn, folding over on themselves, moving ever closer, and the lake water, dark and smooth, seems to lie in wait. Lightning flashes brighter. Thunder claps ever louder. And we wait, too, awed by the spectacle, blessed to be part of it, but just a little afraid of what is to come—for thunderstorms in the Boundary Waters can be vicious,

167

blowing over tents, tearing up trees, starting fires, and soaking equipment.

An even louder clap of thunder. We feel the first drops of rain, big splatters that strike our dusty campsite, bounce off the kitchen tarp, and create little whirlpools on the lake's surface. We crowd under the kitchen tarp as the first gust of wind sweeps across the lake, tearing at the smooth surface, creating waves that pound against the rocks below our campsite.

Lightning flashes turn night into day like someone flicking a light switch: bright light, dense darkness, bright light, dense darkness. The thunder is so loud it seems to shake the bedrock under us, jars our teeth, rattles our senses—and above all impresses us with it vastness, its power.

A wall of rain engulfs our campsite—Paul Bunyan and his crew of giants from the north dumping immense buckets of water on the fragile kitchen tarp, with each corner roped to a tree. The tarp sags, filling with water; I stand and push it up, and water pours off the sides, joining the rest of the deluge that is rushing over the rocks and pouring into the lake. The sound of raindrops on the tarp is near deafening, exceeded only by the claps of thunder that are beginning to diminish now as the storm moves to the east, visiting other lakes, reminding other campers that in the Boundary Waters, nature is indeed still in charge.

Thunder now becomes once more a low growl in the east as the storm quickly moves away. The rain stops as quickly as it started, and except for an occasional raindrop falling from a tree, it is quiet once more. The waves cease splashing, and a great calm moves over the lake. We've been firsthand visitors to one of the Boundary Waters' truly awesome events: a summer thunderstorm in all its fury and glory.

On our trip in 2001, we experienced one of the more memorable storms of our many years in the BWCAW. As we usually did, we checked the weather forecast at the ranger station when we picked up our permits on August 6. The temperature in Madison was predicted to reach 100 degrees, and we looked forward to cooler weather. The weather forecast for the BWCAW: "Lows in the fifties, highs in the seventies each day. Partly cloudy." Perfect weather for a canoe trip.

Tuesday morning we put in on McFarland Lake and then portaged to Pine Lake, where we canoed a good distance and set up our permanent camp. The weather in Madison had been hot and humid, and it felt the same here. I told Steve that a big storm was brewing. His answer: "Dad, you say that every year. Let's go fishing." So we fished, catching one smallmouth bass after the other. I had never seen Pine Lake so smooth—but as the saying goes, "It's not natural."

We turned in early that night after spending the evening in front of the campfire, despite the heat and humidity. No need to worry about being cold in my sleeping bag.

The next morning I crawled out of my tent and looked across the lake. It was glassy smooth, as it had been for the past twelve hours. Red and pink streaked the eastern sky. A pair of loons floated silently a few yards from our campsite. The air was thick and warm. A red squirrel chattered, and a lone mosquito found the back of my hand.

Steve was still asleep in his tent when I heard a deep growl in the west, low and far away. The lake remained calm. A flock of gulls that had spent the night on the rocks a few hundred yards from our campsite lifted up in a mass and flew to the middle of the lake, spacing themselves a dozen or more yards apart. It reminded me of what the navy does when ships are in port and a major storm is forecast—ships head for deep water.

The thunder boomed louder, and the sky continued to darken. I saw the first jagged cut of lightning. Awakened by the thunder, Steve crawled out of his tent. I told him about the gulls, and we sat under the cooking tarp and watched the lightning.

About 7:30 AM the first drops of rain began striking the cooking tarp. They sounded like a drummer warming up, slow, then faster, finding the beat and feeling the music. Raindrops on the lake created hundreds of little circles, each with a tiny echo. More music.

A gust of wind slammed into the tarp, sending it flapping. Thunder boomed all around—west, south, north, overhead. I covered the camp stove with a cooking pail to protect it from the horizontal rain that flew on the wind, soaking everything. Steve and I had already pulled on our waterproof gear. We talked about the July 4, 1999, storm in the BWCAW that blew down thousands of acres of trees. I hoped this was not a repeat. The wind continued to torment our camp, but so far all was well. The tarp, although flapping, stayed in place. The tents appeared secure.

We now saw whitecaps on the lake—long rope-like stretches of froth. Waves pounded on the rocks in front of the campsite, sending up long fingers of spray. I wondered about the gulls and how they were faring. They seemed to know what they were doing.

By 8:30 the wind died down and the waves began subsiding. The whitecaps on the lake disappeared, but the rain continued, steady and soaking. We sat under the tarp, dozing and reading and enjoying the sound of the rain drumming overhead. I started the camp stove and heated some water, and we drank coffee and ate oatmeal. Occasionally Steve stood up and dumped water from the tarp, catching it in a bucket—a few less quarts to boil. Unfortunately, with each dumping, a little more water ran down his sleeve. Fancy rain gear is not designed for dumping and catching water from a kitchen tarp.

By midmorning the rain stopped, but everything was dripping—trees, tarp, my hat. Rain dripped from a big white pine tree that hung over the canoe. The raindrops striking the bottom of the canoe sounded like popcorn popping. A pair of loons floated by. They talked in small yips, like puppies.

Before noon the wind was up again, a stiff breeze from the southwest. Once more, waves beat against the rocks by our campsite. The pine trees were talking in a language of the ancients. The sound of seasonal change was high up in the pines and birch—the sound of fall.

At lunchtime two forest rangers stopped by in a new, lightweight canoe, checking our camping permit. I asked them about the weather forecast. "Maybe another thunderstorm in the afternoon, then clearing." They paddled off. Many more miles to cover, they said, as they headed west into the light chop.

That evening we finished supper, washed dishes, and decided to fish until dark. The air still felt close and humid. The weather front obviously had not yet gone through. We weren't out on the lake more than fifteen minutes when I saw the first slice of lightning in the southwest. I suggested we paddle back to camp, and we did so reluctantly, as the fish were biting. But this was something I'd learned a long time ago: If you see lightning, get off the water as quickly as possible. Boaters and canoeists are easy lightning targets.

Back in camp we stored the canoe high on the rocks and I tied the canoe rope to a tree. As I did this I saw that the storm seemed to have slid around to the south. We watched the lightning show, each flash trying to better the previous. Horizontal flashes, vertical flashes, two vertical flashes together. Steve took pictures. I watched.

At times the lightning in the distance was continuous, lighting the sky like streetlights from a fair-size town. Clouds rolled back on themselves, forming and re-forming. I heard the first thunder. Then more. Soon the thunder was rolling across the lake, tumbling over and over like the clouds.

By 8:30 PM the first drops of rain began falling, and we scurried to our tents. I still believed the main thrust of the storm was to the south and moving away from us. Raindrops beat on the tent roof as I read my book, holding a flashlight with one hand. I was reading *All Quiet on the Western Front* by Erich Maria Remarque, a classic I somehow had missed, its story of World War I echoing the fury and agony of the storm outside my tent.

A flash of lightning illuminated the tent, followed immediately by a ground-shaking roar of thunder. At that moment a gust of wind walloped the tent. I expected it to collapse, the slender poles to buckle, or worse, for the whole thing, me included, to tumble down the bank into the frothy lake. (Later, when I told Steve this, he said it would have been funny to see my tent and me in the lake. So much for his sense of humor.) The rain was falling in torrents. Then it stopped abruptly and the wind was gone. I heard a distant rumble of thunder in the east.

I zipped open the tent flap and stepped outside, expecting our kitchen tarp to be missing, but it was in place. The trees dripped. Steve joined me, and we watched the stars. It was warm, but clear. Good weather tomorrow, I said to Steve.

Later that night something awakened me. It was too hot in the sleeping bag, that must have been it. I made some adjustments. Then I heard a huge explosion of thunder, saw a flash of lightning, and more thunder. Loud thunder. I was reminded of the sounds of the big guns in *All Quiet on the Western Front*.

Now it was continuous thunder and lightning, each assault a little closer until the storm was on top of us. Body-slamming wind shook my tent, the wind stronger by far than in either of the previous storms. I was certain that this time my tent and everything in it were destined to tumble into Pine Lake and float off to the east on the frothy white-caps. The tent protested, fought back, shuddered and shook—and held its ground. Torrential rain beat on the tent's nylon fly, like someone had aimed a fire hose at it. The storm didn't let up. I zipped all

Paddle by a campsite after a heavy rain, and it's easy to spot which tents may have leaked; sleeping bags are hung out to dry.

the tent's zippers and dragged my clothing to the center of the tent. I felt for water dripping from the top and oozing up from the bottom. So far so good. I was still dry.

Finally the wind subsided and the thunder became a distant rumble, but the rain continued, and once more I fell asleep, thinking that come daylight Steve and I would have to search the woods for the kitchen tarp that surely must have torn loose this time.

The next morning I was up early to survey the damage. Every one of my tent pegs had been yanked loose—they lay scattered about. The kitchen tarp was still in place, but the kitchen gear, except for the camp stove, was soaked. I soon had the stove started and was heating water for coffee.

When Steve got up he told me that water had run between his ground cloth and the bottom of his tent, so it felt like he was like sleeping on a waterbed. I shared my worries about lightning striking a nearby tree and showed him my tent pegs scattered about.

That morning both the humidity and the temperature were down. A few remnant storm clouds hurried across a clearing sky. A loon flew over. Sunshine illuminated the trees across the lake. It would be a better day, and we would have yet another thunderstorm tale to tell, with neither of us the worse for wear. Thankfully, our camp gear survived as well. Nothing broken, nothing lost. We were ready to camp another day.

17

Rain

There are thunderstorms with rain, and then there's just plain rain. Wet, driving, dripping, soaking, everything-gets-wet rain. While reviewing my BWCAW journal entries, I saw that no topic has garnered more space than rain.

I've never been one to complain about rain. I grew up on a sandy farm where rain generally made the difference between a crop and the farm making some money—or not. And a rainy day usually meant a day of rest, sometimes an opportunity to go fishing.

Rain is good for the BWCAW, too. It keeps the foliage lush and growing, helps maintain water levels, and keeps forest fires at bay. And rain builds character in the folks who canoe camp there—at least, that's what Steve says. A quick check of Ely, Minnesota, weather records shows an average precipitation of about 20 inches for the six months April to September, and 28 inches for the entire year.

Now this may sound like complaining, but I am stating a fact: of the twenty-five years that we've canoed in the BWCAW, I can think of only one or two years that we didn't have rain (not necessarily a tent-shaking thunderstorm, but some rain).

During our first trip to the area in 1983, I wrote:

Tuesday, August 16, 1983.
About 3 PM it began raining lightly, and it still is. I am
writing this sitting under a big white pine tree. So far so
good, I'm staying dry. Steve is reading in the tent. It's a
relaxing afternoon.

That first year we didn't know enough to hang a tarp over our cooking area, or maybe we couldn't afford it. One of the first things I bought before venturing forth the following year was a 10 x 12 piece of ripstop nylon tarp that we have used every year since. Several of the brass grommets in the corners have pulled out, and now we tie a rope around the end of the tarp. Although not as neat and tidy, the system works just fine to keep the tarp in place, and it keep us dry, mostly, during the rains that visit our camp nearly every year.

Wednesday, July 18, 1990. John Lake
We'd just finished supper when the rains came again.
Thunder and lightning and hail; pea-size hunks of ice
gathered on the rocks before melting. And a downpour
that continued for a couple hours. We huddled under
our green tarp, applauding ourselves that we had sense
enough to purchase one in 1984. It was, as they say
in bad stories, "a dark and stormy night." We heard
a rustling in the bushes, and out of the rain and cold
appeared two hikers. They were wet to their hides,
miserable and cold.
*   We invited them to share our shelter and a cup*
of hot coffee. They said they were hiking the Border

A ripstop kitchen fly we purchased in 1984 has been invaluable over the years. It has kept us dry, mostly, during many rainstorms.

Route Trail and asked if they could pitch their tent at our campsite. Yes, of course, we told them. We had a delightful visit, learned they were from Minneapolis and hiked a lot. They told us about the Border Route Trail, which is 65 miles long and crosses the BWCAW in the northeast corner of Minnesota and follows the international border between Minnesota and Ontario, Canada. We also learned that hiking in the dark, in the rain, is considerably more character building than canoe camping in the rain.

A cold and wet evening with raindrops pounding on the tarp became an interesting one with stories swapped and miseries shared.

Thursday, July 19, 1990. John Lake

Looks like today, finally, we'll be able to dry out our wet sleeping bags and tent. With such a downpour last night, the rain ran under the tent and soaked through *the bottom, which was supposed to be waterproof. Must look into buying a new, more waterproof tent.*

Some years the rain was no more than a quick shower that came up fast, dumped on us, and left as quickly as it came. Other years the rain persisted, like a relative who had worn out a welcome and didn't know enough to leave.

Wednesday, September 6, 2000. 7:00 AM. Pine Lake
Rain. Started about an hour ago. Not heavy. Just a steady drumming on the tarp strung over our cooking area with enough room for sitting, and listening. Nothing sounds better than rain thumping on canvas.

Thursday, September 7, 2000. 7:15 AM. Pine Lake
*This morning I was greeted with a double rainbow over the lake. Quite a sight to see, but also a reminder of what was to come. I remember the old saying, "Rainbow in the morning, sailor take warning." Soon after breakfast, cold rain. Not heavy, but persistent. Pounding on the kitchen tarp. No mosquitoes or black flies. Just the sound of the rain and the loons calling in the distance. A great contrasting sound—raindrops and loon calls. I'm reading Thoreau's **Walden**, as I have many times before. Each reading I gain some new ideas, a different perspective.*

Friday, September 8, 2000. 4:00 PM. Pine Lake
Rain continued all day. Impossible to stay dry. Wind blew up the tarp and the rain blew in. If it were colder it would be even more miserable.

As I read these entries, many years after I wrote them, I'm reminded that even the romance of raindrops begins to disappear when everything is wet. In recent years we have purchased better tents, and each of us has good waterproof rain gear keeping us dry from head to foot, or nearly so. But a sunny day is a welcome day in the BWCAW.

Wednesday, September 3, 2003. John Lake
Woke up to rain. Went to sleep last night to rain. Sharp thunderstorm until about nine. Cold, steady rain this morning. Rain under the tent and soaked into the inside. Gear still dry, however. Rainwater pooled on the kitchen fly. Probably time to buy a new tent, one with a waterproof floor. I've been putting it off. Sun struggling to rise this morning. Gray, gloomy, chilly. Pulled on extra clothes but still not comfortable. Writing hand is cold. Steve still sleeping. A raven calls off to my right, deep in the woods. A cold sound on a wet, dreary morning.

Prepare for rain. Enjoy it. Complain if you must, but it won't help. Rain is a part of the Boundary Waters experience. We've learned to live with it; we also do well without it. Think about this: If every day was a sunny day, how boring that would be.

18

Rough Water

The wind has not always been friendly to Steve and me. When we left Grand Marais early on the morning of September 3, 2002, we noticed a bit of chop on Lake Superior but didn't think much about it. Over the years we have noticed that Grand Marais' weather does not predict well the weather we'll face some 50 miles into the BWCAW.

As we drove along the Sawbill Trail that early morning, with the sun just peeking over the horizon, we talked little as Steve drove and I looked for wildlife—a deer jumping in front of us, or a moose chomping on breakfast in one of the little swamps we drove through. To arrive at Pine Lake and BWCAW entry number 68, we had to canoe the length of McFarland Lake, which has a considerable number of summer cottages and some year-round residents as well. McFarland Lake is an easy lake to canoe, especially in late season, when the fishermen and their boats are mostly absent. When we put in at the landing, we noticed a considerable breeze. It took Steve four or five paddle thrusts before we got under way, but we managed to paddle across McFarland with little difficulty. Soon we were at the short portage that would take us to Pine Lake and then on our way to our favorite campsite, which was about a mile or so from the portage.

Pine Lake is about 8 miles long and a half mile or so wide. It's fairly deep, 80 feet in some places. The lake stretches east and west so the westerly winds, which are most prevalent this time of the year, have a full sweep of it. As we made the short portage from McFarland to Pine, I heard the wind in the treetops but thought little of what we would soon face on Pine Lake. After all, we had faced windy days before and had canoed in chop that challenged us but never defeated us.

Once through the portage, we both stopped and looked with amazement. While there had been a moderate chop on McFarland Lake, Pine Lake was roaring. Whitecaps were rolling as far as we could see up the lake, and waves pounded on the rocks in front of us. The sound of the waves was so loud I had to yell to Steve, "What do you think?"

"Looks a little rough," he replied, a considerable understatement.

We stood watching the angry lake for fifteen minutes or so, not yet loading the canoe. We could see our vacant campsite off to the left, on a rocky point of land jutting into the lake. We could also see the waves sending up sheets of spray as they pounded the rocks below the campsite.

"I think we can make it," Steve said. "We've got a loaded canoe. We'll ride fairly low in the water, so the wind won't bounce us around as much as if we were empty."

"I don't know," I said.

Steve started loading our gear in our Grumman, making sure the load was well balanced and secure. We each put on our life vests, making sure every buckle was buckled, every tie tied, and we set off into the fray. The plan was to canoe close to shore, not so close that we'd be caught and pounded against the rocks, yet close enough that if something happened we wouldn't be far from safety.

Steve took his place in the back of the canoe, I in the front, and we pushed off. Our first challenge was to move away from shore. Each wave worked hard to push us back as the canoe rose and fell, meeting each whitecapped wave head on. Steve is a strong paddler, I less so, but soon we were bobbing and bouncing our way toward our campsite. As we slowly paddled along shore, we quickly discovered that it was even windier than we thought. The deafening sound of the waves crashing on the shore rocks prevented any conversation as we paddled on, each stroke making me at least a little more confident that we'd make it to our campsite with little problem except for some water in the canoe from the occasional wave splashing over the bow. We settled into our paddling routine, now with the wind and waves striking us at an angle as we paddled southwest, one difficult stroke after the other. I was beginning to relax a little; I assumed Steve was, too, as his paddle strokes were sure and even.

Neither of us saw it coming. A rogue wave, perhaps 4 feet high, struck us full force, dumped a load of water in the canoe, and capsized us. The next thing I knew I was in the water, head first. I immediately bobbed to the surface and grabbed the canoe. What we had not tied down in the canoe floated around us, moving with the waves toward shore. The canoe and I bobbed toward shore; I soon discovered I could stand on the bottom of the lake.

"Gotta keep the canoe from smashing into the rocks," Steve yelled as he worked his way around the nearly sunken craft. The sound of the waves crashing on the rocks made it nearly impossible to hear each other. I grabbed a canoe paddle that floated by and snagged a canteen of water. Steve was trying to steer the canoe to shore, among the rocks and waves, as I splashed my way to shore, thoroughly soaked. I managed to retrieve my hat from the turmoil—it was full of water but still floating.

With the canoe finally out and secure, we both hustled to drag our backpacks out of the water, made sure we had both canoe paddles, and realized that one of our canteens had floated away. Having done the best we could to retrieve everything and having made an assessment of our personal injuries—only a few bumps and scrapes from the rocks—I sat down and dumped the water out of my boots. Steve searched for his boots, as he wears sandals when paddling. The wind continued slamming into us, and even though the temperature was in the high fifties and the sun shining brightly, I began to shiver. I was meeting hypothermia head-on for the first time.

Later I did some checking on hypothermia. The Mayo Clinic says this:

> Hypothermia is a medical emergency that occurs when your body loses heat faster than it can produce heat, causing a dangerously low body temperature.

Normal body temperature is around 98.6°F. (37°C). Hypothermia (hi-po-THUR-me-uh) occurs as your body temperature passes below 95°F. (35°C). When your body temperature drops, your heart, nervous system and other organs cannot work correctly. Left untreated, hypothermia eventually leads to complete failure of your heart and respiratory system and to death.[1]

According to the Mayo Clinic, someone experiencing hypothermia usually goes through these stages:

Shivering; clumsiness or lack of coordination; slurred speech or mumbling; stumbling; confusion or difficulty thinking; poor decision making, such as trying to remove warm clothes; drowsiness or very low energy; apathy, or lack of concern about one's condition; progressive loss of consciousness; and weak pulse with shallow breathing.[2]

Steve, a former camp counselor and Red Cross certified in water safety, knew exactly what I was experiencing. I had made a serious mistake, one that Steve had warned me about earlier and now reminded me about again: I was wearing blue jeans. They take forever to dry. Steve wears the synthetic material that is lightweight and dries quickly. I had told Steve that these fancy pants weren't for me, that I could stick with my comfortable blue jeans. Now I wished I had made the switch. (Today I don't climb into my canoe wearing blue jeans. The lesson was well learned).

Steve suggested I take off my wet clothes and hang them on the bushes in the wind and bright sun to dry. Once my skin dried, I began to feel warmer. But we had other problems, of course. We could see our campsite, about half a mile away. But how would we get there? Reloading the canoe and paddling was out of the question, at least until the wind went down. A wind like this could go on for an hour, or it could continue for two days.

Once Steve decided I was okay, he offered to see if he could find his way to our campsite along the shore. But it was impossible to walk along the shore because of huge rocks stacked every which way by the glacier thousands of years ago. Further, huge waves were pounding the rocks, sending spray 6 feet into the air.

He set off through the brush as I sat warming myself in the sun and checking to see what water damage we had to our gear. Thankfully, we had stuffed our sleeping bags into big garbage bags, so they were dry. Our food was in waterproof bags, also dry. The biggest casualty was my billfold and everything in it. Usually I put my billfold in a Ziploc bag, but on this trip I had not. After dumping the water out, I removed my bills—laundered money in the most literal sense—and laid them out on a rock out of the wind but where the sun could get at them. Then came my credit cards, no damage. The little slips of paper where I make notes and keep phone numbers were mostly ruined, the ink running and the paper soggy and fragile. There it was, my personal identification, money, driver's license, various soggy membership cards, all sitting around on rocks, vivid reminders of what I should have done and hadn't.

After fifteen or twenty minutes (my watch was waterproof and still worked fine—one thing I had done right), I looked toward the campsite to see if Steve had made it through the brush. After a half hour had passed I started to become concerned. He was mucking through the brush over steep and rocky terrain with a heavy pack, though in no danger of getting lost, as the roar of the waves on the rocks was always to his right.

Finally I glimpsed him, standing at the rocky outcropping of our campsite, waving. I waved back. I began gathering up my damp clothing. After a half hour in the sun, my blue jeans were far from dry. I reassembled my soggy billfold's contents. My shivering had stopped some time ago, and I pulled on my quick-dry pants, which I should have been wearing all along. I was still far from comfortably warm.

In about twenty minutes Steve was back. In contrast to my predicament, he was sweating—and smiling as he reported that it was obviously possible for us to hike to our campsite, although I might have some difficulty negotiating one of the steep rocky inclines he had encountered.

Steve set off again with the big Duluth Pack, and I continued sitting in the sun.

When Steve returned, we pulled the canoe into the bushes where it would be invisible to anyone paddling by. I shouldered my light day pack and grabbed the fishing poles, Steve slid into the other day pack, and we were off, long-legged Steve in the lead, me stumbling along behind. By the time we had hiked a hundred yards or so I was no longer cold but in fact was becoming steamy warm. Steve tried to retrace his earlier steps but couldn't. The rock-strewn surface, studded with brush and trees, showed little evidence of where he had hiked before. I knew the trip was only about half a mile, and after twenty minutes or so of difficult walking I jokingly asked, "Are we there yet?"

"Hardly," Steve said as he pointed to a near-straight-up incline we had to negotiate. A little stream of water trickled out of the woods and dumped into the lake at the foot of the steep hill. Steve negotiated the hill with little difficulty. I scrabbled my way up, grabbing a small tree and pulling myself up to it, grabbing the next tree, and so on. It was a tree-by-tree climb, one of the most demanding I had ever made, especially wearing a backpack and not having dependable footing.

Once at the top, Steve informed me that we had hiked about halfway to the campsite, but the rest of the trip would be considerably easier. It was. I checked my watch when we arrived at the campsite; the hike had taken forty-five minutes. I slid the pack from my aching shoulders and sat down on a huge rock overlooking the lake. The sun shone brightly, but the wind continued to howl. The sound of the waves crashing on the rocks below the campsite now had become an entertaining sound rather than a menace. On the lake were whitecaps as far as I could see. No sign of seagulls, loons, bald eagles. All had apparently hunkered down for the duration.

After a brief rest, we began unpacking our equipment to assess what had gotten wet besides my billfold and me, and what else we may have lost when we capsized. We had everything except the one canteen. (The next day we looked long and hard for it along the lakeshore, but we never found it.) Our extra clothing, sleeping bags, and food were dry. Unfortunately, I had failed to pack my writing pad and my book, *Songs of the North* by Sigurd Olson, in a plastic bag, and both were soaked. I put the pad and my book on a rock in the sun and hoped for the best. Both eventually dried, but they were crinkled from the soaking. I still have the book on my shelf, a rather ironic remembrance of the event, as Sigurd Olson wrote about canoeing and the dangers of high wind when one is on the water. That week I wrote notes on crinkled paper and read inspiring words from a badly misshapen Olson book, but with the words all intact and in the proper order.

I had remembered to put my canoeing journal, camping permits, maps, compass, and other essential materials in a plastic bag. That night, wearing dry clothes and sitting by a crackling campfire, I wrote in my journal about the adventure and focused on what I had learned from it. The most obvious lesson: Don't mess with Mother Nature. She usually wins, and in this case she surely did. But she was easy on us, mainly just teaching us a valuable lesson. When the waves are high, sit down and wait. It might take six hours; it might take twenty-four. But patience surely trumps a capsized canoe.

Wear a good life jacket, the kind that includes several buckles and straps, that fits and that will pop your head out of the water when you go overboard. Mine also has a little whistle attached to it, as

A lake can be quiet and peaceful with but a few ripples, then a storm surges out of the southwest and waves pound the rocks, keeping canoeists in camp.

well as reflective tape, if, heaven forbid, I should be dumped in the lake at night and someone is flashing a light with the hope of finding me. Wear quick-dry clothing, not blue jeans. Steve did; I didn't. I do now. Learn to recognize the symptoms of hypothermia. You can get hypothermia on a relatively warm sunny day. Ask me.

Don't panic when you find yourself in the water. Life jackets do work well—but they must be worn, not stuffed under a seat in your canoe. Stay with your canoe. Even when it's filled with water, a canoe will float. Hang on to it. Tie your packs and gear to the crossbars in your canoe. We had mostly done that, but had not secured our canteens. When capsized, immediately look for your paddles. The old saying "Up the river in a canoe without a paddle" is right on target.

That night I crawled into my tent with the wind howling through the treetops and waves splashing high on the rocks. I slept soundly and awakened the next morning to complete silence. The lake was as smooth as a shiny tabletop, glistening in the morning sunlight. After breakfast, Steve hiked to where we had stashed our canoe and paddled back to the campsite. Compared to our first day, the rest of the week was uneventful. Since what could have been a very serious accident, both Steve and I have a new reverence for the wind, and a new appreciation for patience.

19
__

Wind and Fire

Anyone who has spent any time in the outdoors
knows that nature is not always peaceful and quiet.
Windstorms and forest fires, both naturally occur-
ring events, raise havoc and can cause tremendous
destruction in a wilderness area like the BWCAW.
Devastating winds can knock over trees, killing
them and creating fuel for a massive forest fire.
According to the US Forest Service, much of the
Boundary Waters Canoe Area Wilderness has been
burned several times in the past. History does not
say whether lightning, Indians, explorers, or traders started the fires—likely some combination of all
of these.

Many people today view forest fires as something that must be controlled at all cost. Yet a fire
can rejuvenate a forest, allowing a new cycle of trees
and other plants to emerge. This rejuvenation can
be beneficial for wildlife, creating favorable habitat
conditions. Of course the problem with a forest fire
is that it can and often does claim human structures.
That's when people complain and demand action,
encouraging Smokey Bear campaigns to stamp out
any sliver of fire in a forest. It's understandable—no

195

one wants to lose his house or shed or even outhouse to a rogue forest fire.

As best I can determine, no one has kept a record of windstorms in the BWCAW. They occur every year in one form or another, usually associated with wicked thunderstorms that boil up in the west and rumble across the northland with a fury that excites, delights, and sometimes causes fear in those who canoe and camp there. They usually come quickly and leave quickly, perhaps knocking down a tent or two, wrenching lose some dead branches, and maybe toppling a few trees before they depart.

The windstorm of July 4, 1999, was much more than a standard summer thunderstorm. Officially known as the Boundary Waters–Canadian Derecho, the storm is commonly referred to as the Boundary Waters Blowdown. *Derecho* is the name given to a fast-moving, intense, and widespread windstorm that is known for its fierce straight-line winds, sometimes reaching 100 miles an hour and more. The storm originated in Montana and western South Dakota and struck Fargo, North Dakota, tearing off roofs and uprooting trees. About 9:30 AM on July 4, the storm, with winds 75 miles per hour and stronger, tore into Bemidji, Minnesota. Weather experts estimated that the storm was moving at 75 to 80 miles per hour when it reached Ely, Minnesota, with surface winds of as much as 115 miles per hour.[1]

According to the Minnesota DNR, the storm destroyed about 400,000 acres in the BWCAW, or about 600 square miles. Many main roads, including the Gunflint Trail, were blocked. Because it was a holiday and a Sunday, many people were camping in the BWCAW. Panic filled the hours following the storm. For several hours no one knew the extent of the storm's damage or the number of injured or possible deaths that had resulted. In its July 5, 1999, edition, the *Duluth News Tribune* gave a sketchy report on the storm damage. Reporters assembled scattered reports of injuries: A person with a spinal injury 8 miles west of the Gunflint Trail; a person with two broken legs just west of Seagull on Alpine Lake; an injured person airlifted from the Brule Lake area.

The Duluth newspaper reported what Jane Mac-Dougall from Duluth had seen while driving on Highway 4 north of Island Lake when the storm hit: "Trees were falling everywhere through an approximately 2-mile stretch hardest hit by the storm. Dozens of trees...I'd say anywhere from 30- to 40-foot pine trees. It looked like something just dug them out from the woods."

The July 6, 1999, issue of the *Duluth News Tribune* reported that fourteen injured campers had been airlifted from the BWCAW, with the search continuing for additional casualties. Forest Service workers did a lake-by-lake, campsite-by-campsite check for the injured, including enlisting the Civil Air Patrol to fly over the area. When they spotted trapped and injured campers, they radioed to floatplanes to rescue them.

First-person accounts by those caught in the storm began emerging. The July 8, 1999, *Duluth News Tribune* carried the story of two campers from Duluth, Glenn Kreag, Barb Koth, and their dog, Abby, who were caught in the storm. When Kreag and Koth saw the storm approaching, they propped their canoe in a tree and crawled under it to eat lunch. Moments later, the storm struck, toppling the tree that held their canoe. Neither was injured, but they knew they needed to find a safer shelter. They crouched under the root-ball of a recently toppled tree, huddling there as trees fell all around them. "It was not like it was huge crashing," Kreag said of the trees. "There was noise from the storm, but the trees bent over and over and over until they gave up. You could just see them going down."

When the storm passed, Koth said, "It was so orderly and at the same time it was utter chaos...I can see why they call them straight-line winds. It is picture-perfect straight-line trees all down in one direction."

Stephen Wilbers, in his "Boundary Waters Chronology," wrote that twenty-five people were injured in the storm, but there were no fatalities.[2] An estimated 32 percent of the BWCAW had been affected, and an estimated twenty million trees toppled, with some trees stacked as high as 20 feet.

Now the Forest Service faced a new problem. With thousands of acres of toppled trees, the risk of a massive forest fire loomed on the horizon. The Forest Service began planning a series of controlled burns to lessen the risk of a catastrophic burn.

Then in the dry spring and summer of 2006, during a thunderstorm on July 14, lightning started a fire near Cavity Lake. The fire spread north to Seagull Lake, near the west end of the Gunflint Trail. Downed trees from the 1999 windstorm provided plenty of fuel for the fire, which began in an area more than a mile from any passable trail.

Toppled trees all around a campsite are evidence that strong winds have swept through the area.

Ada Igoe, a 2006 summer employee at the Gunflint ranger station, wrote this about what became known as the Cavity Lake Fire:

> On Sunday night the fire, producing its own weather, whipped up a windstorm that sent balls of fire flying across Seagull Lake, hopping from one island to the next. Camping latrines melted and lakes filled with ash. On Monday the wind blew in such a way Grand Marais, roughly 35 miles from the burn, filled with smoke, soot falling from the sky.[3]

The fire continued throughout July and into August. Finally, by August 8 fire officials said that 95 percent of the fire had been extinguished. One of the largest fires in the history of the BWCAW, it had burned about 39 square miles of land. No one was injured, and no private property was lost. Ten of the BWCAW's eighty-nine entry points were closed as a result of the fire.[4]

Firefighters had little time to rest, as another major fire erupted in the blowdown area of the BWCAW on May 5, 2007. This fire, known as the Ham Lake Fire, was started by a careless camper who left a campfire unattended. Investigators determined that the fire started at a campsite on Ham Lake and quickly moved northwest, reaching Seagull Lake the following day. The fire burned for more than a week and eventually covered 57 square miles in and near the BWCAW, with an additional 61 square miles burned in Ontario. It destroyed 140 buildings, including ten year-round homes. No one was killed or seriously injured by the flames.[5] The Ham Lake Fire was deemed the most destructive fire in Minnesota since 1918. It moved 12 miles down the Gunflint Trail, destroying structures along the way, including a church-operated camp on Seagull Lake. Forty of the camp's sixty structures burned, including the camp director's home and the hospitality center.[6]

Ironically, the only death related to the Ham Lake Fire was that of the man accused of starting it. Stephen Posniak, a longtime camper in the BWCAW, committed suicide on December 16, 2008, in the backyard of his home. He had been scheduled to stand trial on January 5, 2009, on charges that he had let a campfire grow out of control and that he lied to investigators. For years he had begun his camping trip at the Tuscarora Lodge.[7]

Upon hearing of the 1999 blowdown and the 2006 and 2007 fires, Steve and I camped in unaffected areas. On one of our trips, we saw some of the results of the blowdown, but we did not camp within the area.

During dry seasons, it is especially important to be careful with all fires. Usually during dry times the BWCAW does not allow campfires. There's a reason for the rule, and it's important to follow it. Even though we enjoy campfires as much as the next camper, we always carry with us a small camp stove on which we do our cooking. And during those times when campfires are allowed, we never leave a campsite without first making sure our campfire is out completely. It may take several pails of water to accomplish this, but just one stray spark can cause an inferno in the forest.

As tragic as the effects of wind and fire can be in a wilderness area, they can have redeeming results as well. With death comes new birth—new plants, new trees, a completely new and regenerated forest.

20

The State Bird of Minnesota

I am no fan of mosquitoes, never have been, never will be. Growing up on a Wisconsin farm, I learned about mosquitoes firsthand. I also learned not to let these pesky little buzzing menaces keep me from doing what I want to do, including canoeing in the BWCAW, where they flourish, growing into some of the finest specimens found anywhere on the globe. We all know and respect the fact that the mosquito is Minnesota's state bird.

Northwoods mosquito stories abound. Paul Bunyan, that mythical woodchopper who with his giant blue ox stomped his way across Minnesota, Michigan, and Wisconsin, knew about mosquitoes. One day while Paul and a small group of fellow loggers sat by a campfire eating their supper, a swarm of mosquitoes attacked them. The woodsmen took cover under a giant cast-iron skillet. The hungry mosquitoes drove their beaks clean through the skillet's bottom. The frightened loggers, fearing for their lives, bent the mosquitoes' beaks, immobilizing the bloodthirsty squadron. Finally, all the mosquitoes' beaks had been bent over. But then, much to the sorrow of the hapless loggers, the mosquitoes flew off with their skillet.

Then there is the story of the fellow who was camping in the BWCAW when he awakened to the sound of mosquitoes buzzing. Upon listening carefully, he overheard two mosquitoes arguing. The first one said, "Should we eat him here, or carry him back home to eat?"

"We'd better eat him here," the second one replied. "If we take him home, the big mosquitoes will take him away from us."

Mosquitoes have menaced campers forever, and campers, being thoughtful and innovative folks, have come up with novel concoctions to make life in the outdoors more livable. Mosquito repellents are varied and many. The earliest was a smoky campfire (smoke does keep the pesky critters at bay, but it is a bit impractical while portaging a canoe. By the way, it's difficult to think of a more miserable circumstance than portaging a heavy canoe on a hot day in July with unsteady footing and a swarm of mosquitoes tearing into your exposed flesh because you forgot to apply some repellent.)

Mosquito glazes became popular in the early 1900s. Rather than chasing a mosquito away, a glaze prevented it from penetrating your skin. Horace Kephart mentioned several glaze recipes in his book *Camping and Woodcraft*. One called for 3 ounces of pine tar, 2 ounces of castor oil, and 1 ounce of pennyroyal oil. The instructions for use:

> Rub in thoroughly and liberally at first, and after you have established a good glaze, a little

replenishing from day-to-day will be sufficient. And don't fool with soap and towels where insects are plenty. A good safe coat of this varnish grows better the longer it is kept on—and it is cleanly and wholesome. If you get your face or hands crocky or smutty about the campfire, wet the corner of your handkerchief and rub it off, not forgetting to apply the varnish at once wherever you have cleaned it off. Last summer I carried a cake of soap and a towel in my knapsack through the North Woods for a seven weeks' tour, and never used either a single time. When I had established a good glaze on the skin, it was too valuable to be sacrificed for any weak whim connected with soap and water.[1]

I suspect most present-day Boundary Waters campers would find it a bit unappealing to go seven weeks without washing one's face or hands. So, what Steve and I do, when our schedules allow, is to canoe after Labor Day, when mosquito numbers are slight to nonexistent most years. We do carry mosquito netting, the kind that goes over our hats and keeps the buzzing nuisances away from ears, neck, and face. And we always bring along some DEET products, which we rub on exposed skin when all else has failed. DEET's scientific name, N,N-diethyl-meta-toluamide, sounds a bit off-putting, but it works, creating a barrier that even the most desperate of flying female skin-biters will avoid. Deep Woods OFF!, with about 24 percent DEET content, claims to protect you for as long as five hours. Forget wristbands treated with DEET or citronella—both are essentially worthless for scaring off mosquitoes.

A smoky campfire can keep pesky mosquitoes at bay.

And when campfires are allowed, we still use one to keep any evening mosquitoes at bay. (I've never seen a deer tick in the BWCAW, and I don't want to, because they can be a carrier for the dreaded inflammatory illness Lyme disease. DEET can also protect you from ticks in areas where they are found. Spray clothing around ankles to keep ticks away.)

This is not to say that we haven't had encounters with this famous Minnesota bird.

Sunday, July 14, 1991. McFarland Lake campsite
Our permit was for July 15, so we camped here for the night. We arrived about 5:00 PM. The mosquitoes numbered in the uncountable, and their thirst for blood exceeded anything we had ever experienced. We slept in the back of the Chevy Blazer, leaving a crack in the window for ventilation. That was a serious mistake.

We could not sleep. Mosquito squadrons buzzed like Scud missiles, except the mosquitoes were far more accurate as they found us without difficulty, tapping fresh blood from arms and legs, necks and backs. No body part was safe from the onslaught. I stopped one as it began crawling up a nostril, I suspect the only part of me that had not already been tapped. To the mosquitoes, I must have looked like a rich Texas oilfield with little blood wells tapped into me everywhere.

I tried covering my head with my jacket, but I soon began to perspire. I had to have relief from the heat, and when I yanked off the jacket, the waiting, buzzing menace immediately attacked without so much as a warning flyby.

About midnight, Steve, now desperate, said, "Let's set up the tent." Earlier we'd decided not to unpack the tent so we could start paddling early the next morning. I said, "Let's close the windows and kill the mosquitoes inside instead." Almost immediately the windows began steaming up in the closed quarters. With not enough room for both of us to take the offensive, Steve began a mass killing, pointing his flashlight at the clusters of critters assembled on the truck's ceiling. His first forays netted up to a half dozen per blow. For nearly a half hour Steve swatted mosquitoes. I could feel dead ones and those near dead trembling as they fell on my face.

Slowly the drone of mosquito flight began to ease as the bloodthirsty ranks died in twos and threes. Steve began pursuing single mosquitoes that tried to escape the killer in their midst. About 12:20 AM—Steve kept track of the time—he discovered a cluster of mosquitoes quietly hiding in the front seat, as if waiting for him to turn off his light so they could mount a surprise attack. But their luck had run out. Steve found and dispatched them. "Gotcha," he said with glee.

Finally, we both fell asleep. By first light, we had our canoe in the water, the previous evening now a bad memory.

Everyone who canoes the Boundary Waters has a mosquito story or two—or more—to tell. It's part of the lore of the North.

An afternoon nap after a hard day of reading and resting.

Part IV: Camping Tips

Oh, how can I say this: People need wild places.
Whether or not we think we do, we do.

—Barbara Kingsolver, *Small Wonder*

After many years of paddling and portaging with an aluminum canoe, we bought a much lighter Kevlar model.

21

Canoes

My dad didn't like canoes. Said they were dangerous—too tippy. He was a flat-bottomed wooden rowboat kind of guy. "When you're fishing,"—the only
reason he saw for climbing into a watercraft—"you
want something stable." So when we went fishing—
which wasn't often, as farm work came first—we
always rented a wooden rowboat, one dollar for a
half day. We always rented from the same person
and always fished on Norwegian Lake in central
Wisconsin. The old creaky boat was stable, but
it leaked. One of us boys was always in charge of
bailing out the water in between tossing out fishing lines. It didn't seem to bother our father that
the ancient wooden boat would likely sink without
constant bailing. It certainly wasn't tippy, especially
with the four of us aboard and a couple of inches of
water sloshing around on the bottom.

I was thirty-two before I ever sat in a canoe—my
father's words of warning had been with me since I
was a kid. One summer weekend my boss, Walter,
asked me if I'd like to accompany him and his two
boys, Gary and Gordie, on a camping-fishing trip
to northern Wisconsin. He said he would fish with

his younger son, Gordie, in their boat; his older son, Gary, who must have been fourteen or so at the time, and I would use their canoe, a 17-foot aluminum Grumman. I didn't tell him about my fear of canoes, nor did I reveal that I'd never paddled one.

I soon discovered that Gary knew how to handle himself in a canoe. We fished for two days in the backwaters and little bays of the lake we were on. I learned, much to my pleasant surprise, that the Grumman was perfectly stable. It moved easily through the water, requiring little effort compared to rowing the old wooden flat-bottomed rowboat. And besides that, it didn't leak.

When I returned home that Sunday evening, I had a new respect for canoes, and I developed what has turned out to be a lifelong love affair with them. Soon I owned a 17-foot Grumman. I still have it, more than forty-five years later, and it's as good as new. My Grumman weighs about 85 pounds. Every spring for many years I carried the canoe to the 5-acre pond on our farm, about a quarter mile from the shed where I store it for the winter. I left it there on shore all summer, ready when we needed it.

When my three kids were big enough to paddle, I showed them how. They wondered a little when I suggested they first put on their swimsuits.

I always insist that everyone in a canoe (or any sort of boat) wear a life vest, no matter how good a swimmer the person claims to be. In spite of how much they protested (all three could swim), they wore life vests—the big orange ones that keep you afloat no matter what.

One at a time I sent them out in the pond with

the canoe and paddle and instructed them to tip it over. On this day, I wanted my kids to learn not only how to paddle a canoe, but how to respect it and to gain some experience in what it takes to tip one over.

"Do anything and everything you can to tip it," I said.

"But won't it sink if it tips over?" Steve asked. I showed him the flotation devices tucked under the front and back of the canoe and assured him that, although the canoe might tip over or fill with water, it would never sink.

Steve paddled out first. He stood in the middle of the canoe—something I never let the kids do when we paddled together. He jumped up and down. He made the canoe wobble. It would not tip. I suggested he stand on one edge. Finally the canoe tipped, but still not easily.

Jeff, the youngest, was next. Somewhat lighter and a little shorter than his brother, he couldn't tip the canoe either, until I told him to crawl to one end, stand up, and lean one way or the other. It tipped easily, much to Jeff's surprise. Sue repeated the same exercise with the canoe.

As canoes go, a 17-foot Grumman aluminum canoe is a tank. In my experience, it is one of the most stable and sturdy of canoes. But it will tip, as my kids learned that day at the pond. Like any other watercraft, it must be respected.

Before I knew very much about the Boundary Waters Canoe Area Wilderness, my family and I had many pleasant adventures canoeing the nooks and crannies of our 5-acre pond, larger when the water was high. One of our most memorable events

215

occurred on a sunny August afternoon, when Steve and I decided to paddle around the pond so he could take some pictures. He was the newspaper photo editor for Madison West High School at the time.

We pulled the canoe out of the tall grass, turned it upright, and carried it to the pond. I took a seat in the front, he in the back. He liked the challenge of steering and by this time had gotten quite good at it.

The warm afternoon sun warmed us, but not excessively. It was a cloudless day without a breeze, so the pond's surface was glassy smooth. We pushed off, paddling slowly toward the north end of the pond, where Steve wanted to photograph pond lilies. After a few minutes of paddling, Steve rested his paddle and adjusted his camera.

"Dad, we've got a problem," he said quietly. "A big problem."

Steve was not one to excite easily. Sitting in the front of the canoe, I couldn't see what he saw.

"There's a snake in the canoe and it's coming your way."

"A snake," I said.

"Oops—two snakes coming your way."

Steve was holding his feet up as he spoke. I turned to look, and sure enough, a pair of garter snakes was sliding across the bottom of the canoe, moving toward the front.

"What should I do?" Steve asked.

"Take your paddle and toss them in the water," I said. I did not relish sharing the front of the canoe with a pair of snakes.

After two or three tries for each snake, Steve managed to toss them into the pond. Later we discovered that a nest of garter snakes had found a home under the rear seat of the canoe. After that experience, each time before launching the canoe we pound on the backseat to dislodge any snakes that have taken up residence there.

It was this well-experienced 17-foot Grumman that we took to the Boundary Waters in 1983. We continued doing so for many years after. Of course the BWCAW is canoe country, says so right in the title.

Canoes in one form or another have been around for thousands of years. The word comes from *kenu*, meaning "dugout."[1] North American Native people developed the popular canoe, which consisted of wooden ribs covered with birch bark. The birch tree was common in many places in the north, and its bark was lightweight, waterproof, and quite strong.

With today's materials and manufacturing techniques, modern canoes are ever more strong and durable. My Grumman has a capacity of about a thousand pounds, which took care of our needs quite well. From 1983 to 2003 we paddled and lugged our Grumman throughout the BWCAW. We rammed into stones, got hung up on underwater trees, and shot through rapids. And I suspect if we added up all the portages we'd made with the Grumman, it would total hundreds of miles. It was because of the portages that Steve one day said quietly, "Dad, any chance that we might buy a different canoe?"

I wasn't surprised—though I was fussy about what kind of canoe should replace the Grumman, which in a way had become a part of the family. I wanted a canoe that would do everything the Grumman did and of course weigh less. Steve and

I occasionally attended canoe shows, and we had watched the development of the new lightweight Kevlar canoes. At Madison's Canoecopia show in spring 2003 we spotted a canoe that caught our fancy, and we bought it. Our new canoe is a 17-foot Kevlar Wenonah Spirit II. It's 36 inches wide at its widest point and weighs 54 pounds, some 35 pounds lighter than our Grumman. *Canoe & Kayak* magazine tested it and concluded that "this canoe is simple and functional. If you could have only one canoe to serve all your needs for the rest of your life, the Spirit II would be one of very few candidates." The promotional material for the canoe says, "At 17' long, it strikes a good balance between the efficiency of a longer hull and the maneuvering of a shorter one. The Spirit II is safe and roomy, too, with the capacity for medium-long trips. With two large people it draws just 4 inches, leaving lots of reserve buoyancy for gear. Loaded it becomes more stable yet still handles well, even on waves."

We are happy with our choice, although a Kevlar canoe can be a bit pricey. We paid about $1,900 for ours in 2003. Of course, I couldn't help comparing the price with what I paid for my Grumman in 1964, which was $350.

Our Wenonah serves us well. Neither Steve nor I are as light as we once were, yet our Wenonah rides well in the water and paddles easy. We're a little more cautious about not striking stones than we were with the Grumman. But the new canoe has its share of scrapes and scratches after six years of paddling, and it doesn't appear to have suffered too much. With a built-in wooden portaging yoke and its lighter weight, the Wenonah makes our portages much more manageable. We also like the farm-machinery type seats that provide more back support than a flat seat.

A few years ago we purchased aluminum paddles with tough plastic blades. I resisted at first—after all, paddling should be done with wooden paddles, the material of choice for hundreds of years. But we have broken a couple of wooden paddles and worn out several more (our fault, as we used the blade ends to push off from rocks a few times too many). Our new paddles are tough, lightweight, and comfortable to use.

After one rather serious dunking and several close calls, we know why it's important to wear life vests whenever we are in the canoe. Don't rely on a cheapie from a box store; good ones cost a hundred dollars or more. Today I use a Lotus Designs vest, Type III PFD, extra large so I can wear a jacket, rain gear, or sweatshirt underneath it. The vest is designed so I can easily paddle while wearing it, and it weighs less than 2 pounds.

New and improved equipment will keep arriving in stores and catalogs. But I'll never sell my old Grumman canoe—it has too many memories. I'll paddle it around my pond at the farm and think about the many years that it provided transportation in the BWCAW. And today I often think of my introduction to canoeing, way back in the mid-1960s, and how I had to overcome my dad's voice in my head, "Never trust a canoe. They're not safe." Today there is little that is more pleasant to me than sliding through the water in a canoe, paddling quietly, leaving behind just a ripple, and doing all this with scarcely a sound.

Tents have been special to me ever since I was a kid. The sound of raindrops on a tent fly is a most pleasurable sound.

22

Tents

When I was ten years old, I desperately wanted a tent. During World War II we had little extra money, although my dad did give me twenty-five cents a week for doing chores—a handsome sum of money in those days, when most farm kids worked on their home farms for no pay. Neither Dad nor Mother had heard of the idea of an allowance; the twenty-five cents was my salary for doing chores.

I spent much of a winter and into the spring paging through the Sears, Roebuck and Company and Montgomery Ward catalogs, looking at tents. Today we'd call them backyard tents. When I had saved the five dollars needed, I filled out an order to Montgomery Ward for a little umbrella tent. I'd decided that with that tent I could do just about everything, including spending many nights outdoors under the stars, surrounded by the sounds of the night.

The tent never arrived. I eventually got a note from the catalog company saying in effect that because of the war effort, canvas was in short supply, especially canvas for tents. My longed-for tent was unavailable. My dream was dashed, but not my love for tents. That love continues to this day. A tent is a special place for me, a mystical place, a place that evokes thoughts of people who used tents long before recorded history.

Armies used them; they still do. Miners lived in tents. Tents provided shelter for pioneers before they could build cabins on their new land. The traveling circus created a veritable tent city when it came to town, with the largest tent, the big top, providing cover for the circus's extravagant shows. Of course the voyageurs, who paddled and portaged throughout the Boundary Waters and elsewhere, lived in tents.

Horace Kephart, the venerable outdoorsman of the early twentieth century, wrote this in 1917 about selecting a tent:

> Wherever transportation is difficult it is imperative that the tent should be light, compact to carry, and, if you are to make camp and break camp every day or so, it must be so rigged that it can be set up easily and quickly by one or two men. The tent should shed heavy rains and stand up securely in a gale."[1]

Kephart's words remain good advice today, especially for canoe campers who are on the move.

Nothing spoils a camping trip quicker than a leaky tent, one that allows mosquitoes inside, or one that collapses in a brisk wind. A wet sleeping bag, wet clothing, mosquito bites, and a tent collapsed on top of you will quickly change a pleasant outing into a disaster.

A few years ago, when I was teaching at the University of Wisconsin and doing leadership workshops for higher-education professors, I took a group of department heads, assistant deans, and other hard-striving junior administrators on a canoe camping trip from Garrison Dam on the Missouri River in North Dakota to a spot north of Bismarck, a distance of about 40 miles. The group consisted of fifteen men and fifteen women ranging in age from early thirties to midforties. They came from all over the United States. More than half of the group had not been in a canoe, nor ever slept in a tent.

Before we left for North Dakota, I sent each of them a list of camping supplies they should bring: sleeping bag, tent, hiking boots, camping clothing, mosquito repellent, that sort of thing. I suggested they not buy the cheapest tent or sleeping bag, as we would be traveling in challenging conditions, canoeing on the river and camping for several nights. (We camped every night at the Lewis and Clark campsites, used by those intrepid explorers as they made their way from St. Louis up the Missouri River and farther west.)

After the first day of canoeing, when most of the tents were up, I walked through our little tent city on the banks of the Missouri, offering suggestions for tent pitching and advising not to forget pounding tent pegs securely. Most new tents will stand without the tent pegs, but they will also blow over, or even blow away, if not fastened down properly.

I saw the most diverse collection of tents I'd ever seen, including several from big box stores that stood tall enough to stand up in, required a long time to erect, and appeared not at all stable. I was more than a little concerned at what I was seeing and wondering if my earlier written communication hadn't been clear about what kind of tent to purchase. Clearly some in my group had gone for the $29.95 backyard-model tents. I had brought a two-person L.L. Bean backpacking tent that I used for camping in the BWCAW. It was light (about 6 pounds), low to the ground (less than 4 feet high at the peak), and had lots of room for one person and gear. It included a weatherproof fly that formed a small vestibule at each end of the tent, and the tight mesh windows and doors allowed ventilation but kept away bugs no matter their size. I paid a couple hundred dollars for it.

The second day on the river was hot and sultry, the kind of weather that produces thunderstorms. That evening we sat around the campfire talking about what we'd seen that day along the Missouri and what the group was making of the adventure so far. I suggested that we all prepare for a storm with heavy rain and wind. Some appeared too tired to care; a few heeded my warning and checked their tents before retiring.

Shortly after midnight I was awakened by the rumble of thunder and a flash of lightning. The thunder rolled down the river, echoing as it traveled north to south. Lightning continued to flash. Within minutes our tent city was plummeted by strong winds and a downpour of rain.

My tent stood firm and dry. I heard a few yells but knew there was little I could do until the storm moved on. In less than a half hour, I emerged from my tent with flashlight in hand to find some tents down, others tipped over, and a group of considerably less-than-happy campers. Many were wet, and some were visibly shaken. No one had been hurt. But about half of the tents, especially the cheap ones, had collapsed, soaking the occupants and the tents' contents. Folks found dry clothes, doubled up with other campers, and got through the night without further problems.

I certainly hadn't planned it, but I was teaching leadership strategies on this trip, and I could think of no better way for my participants to learn about adversity than to face it personally with its obvious discomforts. Over the years I have heard from some of these unhappy campers, many of whom went on to administrative positions in major universities. "That night on the Missouri River taught me a lot about myself" is the theme I heard many times over. Still, I wouldn't wish that kind of experience on anyone, and there is no need for it as long as you purchase proper equipment.

For my first camping trip in the BWCAW, I borrowed a four-person Eureka tent from my neighbor. Upon returning home, I bought a four-person Eureka Timberline tent that served us well for many years. I have learned a thing or two about tent size ratings: A two-person tent is mighty cozy for two people, with little room to store clothing and other gear. A four-person tent is even more crowded with four occupants. Our four-person Eureka worked fine for Steve and me and even sufficed for three campers for a few years. But then a strange thing happened. I noticed that each morning I was waking up with sore ribs. When I complained to Steve about it, he said he couldn't figure out why that would be—perhaps my air mattress wasn't inflated properly. The problem continued until one morning, Steve, with a big smirk on his face, fessed up: when I started snoring, he'd elbow me in the ribs to wake me up.

The next year we solved the sore ribs problem. Steve bought his own tent, I bought my own tent, and we pitched them a considerable distance from each other. No more sore ribs, and now Steve gets a good night's sleep. My new L.L. Bean two-person tent worked fine for me, while Steve bought a North Face three-person all-season tent that he could use both in the BWCAW and for winter camping. His new tent was similar to a style he had used on several mountain climbing trips: easy to set up, able to withstand strong winds, waterproof, and breathable.

Some years later, when my Bean tent had seen better days, I bought a three-season REI half-dome four-person tent, with a 51-inch peak and 94 x 86-inch footprint. It weighs about 5 pounds and has but two poles, which makes it easy to erect. The tent has two vestibules where I keep much of my equipment out of the weather, and two doors. I appreciate the head room, as I enjoy sitting in my tent on a folding camp chair when it's raining. And on those evenings when hungry mosquitoes fill the air, I sit in my tent and read. These days I also use a folding cot that allows me plenty of room for everything, high and dry and protected from the BWCAW's fierce storms.

Aside from the practical aspects of tent size, shape, weight, and cost, a tent is much more for me than a roof over my head—although of course that is important. My tent ties me to the outdoors and yet provides an opportunity to live in nature in relative comfort. My tent offers sounds and smells replicated nowhere in our modern world. I believe we all have a need for wilderness, a desire to go back in time and experience what those who came before us experienced. A tent allows that to happen.

The sum total of our cooking gear today. Each year we have left a few more kitchen items at home.

23

Equipment and Clothing

In 1917 Horace Kephart wrote:

> To be sure, even though a man rigs up his own outfit, he never gets it quite to suit him. Every season sees the downfall of some cherished scheme, the failure of some fond contrivance. Every winter sees you again fussing over your kit, altering this, substituting that, and flogging your wits with the same old problem of how to save weight and bulk without sacrifice of utility. All thoroughbred campers do this as regularly as the birds come back in spring, and their kind has been doing it since the world began. It is good for us. If some misguided genius should invent a camping equipment that nobody could find fault with, half our pleasure in life would be swept away.[1]

Kephart had his finger on the truth of the matter. After many years of camping, I still pore over camping magazines and equipment catalogs every year. Steve and I continue to flog our wits at the end of each season as to what worked well, what we must replace, and what to add to our camping outfit. We

When purchasing camping equipment, buy strong canvas packs. We've used the same Duluth Packs for nearly twenty-five years, and although they're a bit faded, they still serve us well.

constantly worry about weight and bulk. We fuss over whether everything will fit in our packs and in the canoe. We mull over weight as much as we fuss about bulk, especially when we plan a trip with a considerable amount of portaging.

Over the years, we've worn out or switched camp stoves four times. We began with a Coleman Peak stove that met our needs for several years, and eventually we replaced that with several lighter, easier-to-use, mixed-gas models.

I'm on my fourth tent. We have our second canoe. I didn't keep a record of the number of paddles we've broken or worn out. We quickly decided after the first trip to buy more comfortable packs. We now leave equipment at home that we once thought essential, such as boat cushions and fancy kitchen equipment. And we've added a few things as well, such as comfortable chairs and even a folding table. Below is our current equipment list, in several categories:

FOR TOTING

PACKS

My first year in the BWCAW, I carried equipment in my old army duffel bag. After the first 50 yards, I unhappily discovered the duffle bag was not designed for portaging. It was clumsy, and the shoulder straps dug into my shoulders. The next year I bought two canvas Duluth Packs with wide leather shoulder straps. We've used at least one of them every year since. Each is 26 inches high, 28 inches wide, and 6 inches deep. In one we pack our food and related cooking equipment; in the other go sleeping bags, clothing, and miscellaneous equipment. Neither has as much as a rip or a tear; they're a bit faded from the sun but are still as serviceable as the day I bought them. The food pack, which we hoist up into a tree to keep bears and red squirrels away, is a bit more tired than the other pack, because it has survived as many thunderstorms as we have. But our food has never gotten wet.

A few years ago I bought a Duluth Pack Sparky Bag, which is designed for day trips. It is 17 inches high, 13 inches wide, and 5 inches deep. Also made of canvas, with padded leather shoulder straps, this little pack opens fully for easy packing and unpacking. In it I carry our first aid kit, extra flashlight, rain gear, and fishing box, and when we are doing day-trip canoeing, our lunches.

I carry a fanny pack in which I keep our maps, permits, a flashlight, matches (waterproof and windproof), binoculars, keys, billfold (in a plastic bag), and other small items.

I also have a waterproof bag, fairly small, in which I pack my clothing, books, writing materials, and anything else that must not get wet. Steve brings along his mountain climbing pack filled with much of his personal equipment.

TRAVELING EQUIPMENT

COMPASS AND MAPS

I can't stress it enough: a good map is essential. And a decent compass helps to solve arguments such as, "Which way did you say is north?"

GPS EQUIPMENT

I own a handheld GPS unit. I leave it at home, in the same category as an electronic fish finder. I'm here in the Boundary Waters to escape technology. So I'm not able to mark a favorite fishing place, and I may get lost on occasion. After all, this is a wilderness area, not a fancy fishing resort.

BINOCULARS

I bring along a pair of Bausch & Lomb Custom 7x26 binoculars that I use for spotting campsites, looking for portages, spying on canoeists that paddle by in the middle of the lake, and checking on loons, eagles, and other wildlife. I've tried other compact binoculars, but these, designed for bird-watching, work best for me. When I'm not using my binoculars, I keep them in a zip-top plastic bag to make sure they don't get wet.

CAMERAS

Since digital cameras became popular, I bring along a pocket-size point-and-shoot model. Because Steve is a professional photographer and has his professional cameras along, I know we'll have a good photo record of our trips in my own Boundary Waters album. As I do with the binoculars, I store my camera in a zip-top bag when I'm not using it.

ROPE

During our first camping trip we learned that we need plenty of rope of various lengths. I like braided polypropylene rope. It's soft, doesn't tangle, is easy to tie, and is tough. I have pieces 50 feet long, 25 feet long, and 10 feet long. It seems no matter how much rope I bring along, we find some way to use all of it.

FOOD STORAGE

We use our large food bag for both toting and storing. Here is the US Forest Service's advice for storing food to keep bears away from your camp:

> Bears have an excellent sense of smell and may be attracted to the food and scented toiletries you carry into the wilderness. To ensure a successful trip, keep these items out of bear's reach. Never leave your food on the ground when you're out of camp, and don't sleep with food in your tent at night. Instead, hang it up high, away from your sleeping area.

The pamphlet goes on to illustrate Method A and Method B for keeping the bears at bay and your food supply intact.

Method A (uses two 50-foot lengths of rope). Rope
#1: Secure a weight (such as a rock) to one end and
throw it over a tree limb. Tie off unweighted rope
end around tree trunk. Throw weighted end over
second limb, and tie it off around second trunk.
Rope #2: Secure a weight to one end and throw
it over rope #1. Wrap horizontally and vertically
around food bag. Raise bag off the ground at least
10 feet, and tie rope off around trunk.

Method B (uses one 50-foot length of rope). Secure
a weight (such as a rock) to one end of rope, and
throw it over a tree limb at least six feet out from
the trunk. Tie rope horizontally and vertically
around food bag. Raise bag off the ground at least
10 feet, and tie rope off around trunk. Bag must
hang at least 4 feet below limb.

Got all that? Nothing to it? On our first camping trip to the BWCAW, we studied methods A and
B at length. Method A, besides being impossible to
understand, required 100 feet of rope, which we did
not have. On to Method B. It sounds simple enough:
Toss a rope over a tree branch, tie the other end to
the food bag, and pull it up.

The first challenge was tossing a rope over a tree
branch at least 15 feet from the ground. An even
weightier challenge was figuring out how to tie a
stone to a rope that can be tossed over a branch. The
first time we tried it, the stone went flying off into
the lake and the rope fell limp in front of me. The
second time, the stone stayed tied, but my toss was
off target and the rope became tangled in an inap-
propriate branch. A half hour later, the rope was

free, my patience shattered, my religion lost, and my son bent over with laughter.

Some version of that first experience takes place every year. There simply is no quick and easy way to toss a rope over a tree branch high overhead. And even when it is done, horsing the food bag up 10 feet with a skinny rope is no easy task. But—and I'll grant you, this is not graduate-level physics—here is how we do it. One guy holds the rope, the other holds the bottom of the food bag, and on the count of three, the guy with the rope pulls and the guy with the food bag pushes. It works—sometimes.

Once the bag is in the air, we tie the rope around the tree and we are bear-safe—or at least we like to think so.

CAMPSITE EQUIPMENT
Cot

I gave up on air mattresses long ago. Too many times I woke up with a deflated mattress and a backache. Twenty years ago I bought a portable cot with aluminum side rails, a canvas cover, and four steel legs that fit into the side rails. The cot is 72 inches long, 24 inches wide, and 6½ inches high. It fits nicely into a canvas traveling case and weighs about 5 pounds. Much fancier and considerably more expensive cots are now available. But mine has served me well, and I see no need to change.

Because the cot is well off the tent floor, I don't have to worry about a wet sleeping bag if water should seep into the tent. Plus, the space under the cot gives me one more place to store stuff. About five years ago I purchased a self-inflating mattress and a self-inflating pillow for the cot. I now sleep in ultimate comfort.

SLEEPING BAG

Choosing a sleeping bag is very much a matter of personal preference. What kind to buy? What covering? What kind of insulation? Mummy bag or a regular one? Weight? How much room does it take up when packed?

Most of us know how we like to sleep. Some of us like it cool, some (like me) like it warm. Waking up shivering in the middle of the night is not something I enjoy, and it has happened to me more than a time or two.

The prices and the quality of sleeping bags vary greatly. My first bag was a loser, except for its price. Today, I have a mummy-type bag insulated with a synthetic material and a temperature rating of plus-20 degrees. One thing I've learned about temperature ratings: buy a bag that's rated 15 degrees lower than you think you need. (I wish I had purchased a bag with a 5-degree rating. When we've camped in September and the temperature sinks into the low thirties, my bag is not warm enough.)

Steve has a mummy-type bag insulated with goose down and a temperature rating of minus-5 degrees. He usually complains about being too warm. A word on goose down compared to synthetic insulation materials: Goose down is more expensive than the synthetic materials, but I believe it is warmer. Goose down also packs into a smaller bundle than synthetic bags do. But if a goose down bag gets wet, its insulation value plummets to nearly nothing, while a wet synthetic bag continues to insulate well.

When I'm ready to store my sleeping bag in the off-season, I take it out of the stuff bag and store it in a big plastic storage box. Some of the bag's loft seems to disappear if I store it in the stuff bag.

Before shoving my sleeping bag into my Duluth Pack, I put it in a big garbage bag to make sure it stays dry along the way.

FURNITURE

For the last ten years or so, we've brought along two folding chairs, the lightweight kind with canvas covers and aluminum frames. I also have a three-legged camp chair that we mostly use while cooking. It saves a lot of squatting and keeps the cook smiling and less grumpy.

A couple years ago I bought a small folding camp table. It's 19 inches square, 18 inches tall, and weighs about 4 pounds. The top is nylon/polyester mesh. Basically, it's a flat place to set stuff. I also use the table for journal writing. I know, I'm supposed to adjust to the environment, which I mostly do, but this little table makes the adjustment a little easier.

CLOTHING

Once more I look to Horace Kephart for advice. He wrote, "The chief uses of clothing are to help the body maintain its normal temperature and to protect it from sun, frost, wind, rain and injuries."[2] Note that he says nothing about style or creating a proper canoeing image. I have seen a few stylish canoeists, those who wore the most up-to-date L.L. Bean, Cabela's, Columbia, or Filson outdoor wear.

Most canoeists—and I would put myself in this category—worry not a wit about style (except for a hat) and are most concerned about comfort. Here are a few things I've learned over the years.

For me, canoe-camping hats are special. A good hat not only prevents sunburn and keeps my head dry when it rains, it also makes an outdoor fashion statement.

HATS AND CAPS

You've got to have a good hat, not only to shield your eyes and keep your head from becoming sunburned, but because a good hat is cool (a contradiction to what I said above about showing off—I do show off with my hat). It makes a fashion statement, declaring to other canoeists that I know about canoeing and I know about selecting hats. Hats are easy to find; most sporting goods store have scads to choose from. I like a hat with a floppy brim and a chin strap. There's nothing worse than having a gust of wind lift your hat from your head and dump it in the lake, requiring a turnaround to retrieve it. Presently I wear a Tilly's hat, but I have worn a Filson for several years. (We canoeists do like to drop names when it comes to hats.)

I also have a cap, the kind with a flap that comes down over my ears and neck to prevent sunburn. It does the job. But it's not near as cool as a good hat.

Finally, I wear a stocking cap on cold nights while I'm sleeping. Somewhere I read that if the top of your head gets cold, you're in trouble.

UNDERCLOTHING

For cool and often wet conditions, I've learned to avoid cotton. Steve's mountain climbing outfitter says, "Cotton kills." There's no cotton clothing allowed on mountain climbing expeditions. But I like my cotton underwear, so I violate the "no cotton" rule. Steve insists that the synthetic materials are comfortable and dry more quickly.

I always bring along long underwear—for this I use synthetic material—the two-piece kind, which works wonders on a cold, windy day or at night when the temperature drops near freezing and I wish I'd spent a few more bucks for a warmer sleeping bag.

I like socks that are a wool-nylon mix, more wool than nylon. They wick away moisture and provide a bit of cushion on long portages, especially when I am carrying a heavy pack. I bring along a couple changes of socks.

BOOTS AND SHOES

Sporting goods catalogs include several pages of hiking boots, with prices ranging from inexpensive to outrageous. Selecting a pair of boots is a personal thing, just like picking out a hat; except I want comfort and safety when I'm hiking, so I care little about the appearance of my boots. I have a moderately priced pair of all-leather boots with a GORE-TEX liner, which makes them waterproof. They have rugged tread for good traction and look like they've been on many a portage (they have).

I'm a dry-foot canoeist. Thankfully, Steve is not. He is the one in the water, keeping the canoe from cracking into a stone when we are pulling into a portage or our campsite. He wears sandals in the water and boots in camp. I wear boots in the canoe and sandals in camp.

My camp sandals are open in the back but have solid toes—too many opportunities for stubbed toes in the BWCAW rocky campsites.

I will quickly admit that my boots are heavier than these lightweight models—mine also are 7 inches tall to prevent ankle injury—but they are comfortable and work well. I learned from my father many years ago to never go on a long hike in new shoes. No matter what the manufacturer might say, a new pair of boots or shoes needs breaking in. The last thing you want on a canoe trip is a blister on your foot.

RAIN GEAR

I don't skimp on rain gear—no cheap plastic stuff that stiffens in the cold and tears with the least contact with brush, twigs, or a hundred other things one runs into while camping. I have learned to buy gear that is completely waterproof—GORE-TEX works, but there is other waterproof rain gear that breathes. I have both a rain parka with hood and rain paints that zip up on the side a few inches so I can pull them over my GORE-TEX–lined boots. My current rain gear is REI brand, but there are several manufacturers of good rain gear. My gear folds up nicely and fits into my daypack, where it is always handy. Rain showers in the BWCAW can come up quickly, dump tons of rain, and then move on. Or an all-day rain lingers and you live in your rain gear— but at least you are dry and mostly comfortable.

PANTS

For several years I canoed wearing my trusty blue jeans (I live in them most of the year, whether I'm working in my garden, chopping wood, or writing). Steve introduced me to lighter-weight, quick-drying pants. He said my blue jeans weighed too much and dried too slowly because they were made of cotton. Of course, I didn't listen. The fateful year we swamped the canoe, I learned the hard way about denim pants that don't dry, ending up in the early stages of hypothermia because of my wet clothes, especially my slow-drying blue jeans.

Today I wear quick-drying nylon pants, the kind with zippers on the legs that allow you to convert the pants into shorts on a warm day. Another plus: These quick-drying pants can be rolled into a little ball and take up almost no room in my clothing bag.

SHIRTS

One thing about BWCAW weather: It is not boring. One day it may be 90 degrees with high humidity; a day later, after a storm front comes through, the early morning temperature may be in the forties with a stiff breeze. I bring along a couple of nylon, ventilated, quick-drying shirts for the warm days. I always pack long-sleeved shirts for protection both from the sun and from bloodsucking, skin-biting, marauding bugs.

COLD WEATHER GEAR

I pack a fleece jacket and fleece vest for cooler days. In early autumn, I also wear a heavy cotton chamois shirt around camp. I bring along a sweatshirt with a hood, which I wear while sleeping on chilly nights and all day when the wind is up and the temperature is down.

When we camp in September, I tote along a light-weight down-filled vest, which is a welcome addition to my layers of clothing in challenging weather. I carry a pair of woolen gloves, which makes life more pleasant on cool mornings.

TOILETRIES

One of my best investments (and inexpensive, too) was a small, canvas fold-up washbasin. I dip it in the lake to fill it, carry it to a handy rock, and enjoy my morning and evening ablutions. I keep toothbrush, toothpaste, and soap in a plastic bag. I purchased a quick-drying face towel some years ago that, indeed, does dry more quickly than the regular kind. I bring along two or three half rolls of toilet paper—one in the food bag, one in my fanny pack, and one in my day pack.

Miscellaneous

First Aid Kit

From the first time we visited the BWCAW, we've always carried a first aid kit. Early on it amounted to some burn lotion, some Band-Aids, and a bottle of aspirin. Today our first aid kit is packed in a water-proof plastic box and includes an array of items, from sterile dressings to triple antibiotic ointment. It's about the size of a paperback book and considerably lighter. We've been fortunate over the years (we're also careful) to have incurred no major burns, cuts, breaks, or other injuries. The first aid kid it there just in case. While camping in the BWCAW, out of range of cell phones and hours away from a doctor, a minor injury can quickly become major if not prop-erly cared for. I am also lucky that Steve's early camp counseling experience included advanced Red Cross first aid training.

Camp Lights

Back in the 1980s, candle lanterns provided our light. They are still available, and they are truly nos-talgic, but they cast little light. The weakest flash-light will do better. For a few years we carried a propane-fueled lantern with a mantle: wonderful light, bright enough for reading, but too fragile. A bump shattered the mantle and left us in the dark. I brought along spare mantles, but it was a hassle to replace them.

Today I have two small LED flashlights. They cast a bright light, and the batteries last much longer than the older flashlights did. I also have an LED lan-tern, which can be operated on low or high power, casts enough light to read by, and is lightweight and sturdy. I keep one flashlight in my fanny pack at all times, for emergencies and so I will always know where to find it.

MOSQUITO DISCOURAGEMENT

In recent years Steve and I have discovered the best way to avoid mosquitoes is to canoe in late August and September when their numbers are few. Some years, if it has been a warm and wet summer, we still encounter a few of the hungry buggers. I have four levels of defense. First, we try to select a campsite that is on high ground and faces the south or west, so any available breeze will sift into camp. Mosquitoes do not like breezes, even light ones.

If fires are allowed, we use a smoky fire to chase away mosquitoes. (Unfortunately, a smoky fire can be as disagreeable as a horde of mosquitoes—camper's choice.)

Several years ago I bought a Bug Out brand jacket, made of fine mesh, with elastic at the sleeves and a hood that fits over my hat so that my face and neck are covered. It contains no chemical repellents. It is loose enough that I can do whatever needs doing without any problem—although staring through the mesh may bother some who insist on clear vision at all times.

Lastly, when the mosquito hoards are so devastating that nothing seems to deter them, I smear on some 100 percent DEET. I always have a small container of DEET in my fanny pack.

For woodcutting we use a fold-up saw. We do not carry an ax or a hatchet—too dangerous, and too heavy to tote.

WOODCUTTING EQUIPMENT

We do not carry an ax or a hatchet with us—too heavy, and too dangerous. I carry a small Oregon brand saw, with a 5½-inch blade that folds into the handle. When open, the blade locks into place, making it a reasonably safe tool to use. I use it for cutting small dead branches and driftwood, which we often use for our campfires (when fires are allowed).

DUCT TAPE

Duct tape will fix just about anything that needs fixing, from a tear in your tent to a hole in your canoe. We bring along a big roll. We've learned to keep it out of the sun; if you leave it in the sun, it'll melt, becoming impossible to use.

24

What's There to Eat?

When we're provisioning for an upcoming trip to the Boundary Waters, we don't spend a lot of time working on menus or planning what we're going to eat. We simply look at the previous year's food list, check for any suggestions for change we've noted, and buy our food a day or so before we leave. I'm fully aware of the gourmet camp cooks who pride themselves on coming up with wonderful main courses and tasty desserts. I know about those who bake bread in reflector ovens and carry wine in old-fashioned wineskins. We do not belong to that group. Having said that, we do eat well, and we enjoy our simple meals.

Over the years we have tried various kinds of cooking utensils and equipment. We've especially focused on our camp stove, an essential item.

CAMP STOVES

I suspect the purists reading this will say, "Why don't you build a fire in the campsite grill and cook your food that way?" The quick answer is that half the time we've been in the BWCAW, campfires have been banned. Without a camp stove, we'd have been eating cold food the entire week. Cold food I could handle, but I couldn't make it without a hot cup of coffee.

In the early years, we used gasoline-fueled stoves. No more—they're too messy and too smelly. More recently, we've used mixed-fuel stoves of various types. For the last couple years we have used a Jetboil stove, which consists of three parts fastened together: a 32-ounce canister for heating water, soup, etc.; the stove; and the mixed-fuel canister on the bottom—one tidy unit. Without question, this is the best camping stove to come along in a while. The manufacturer claims this little wonder will boil water in a minute. Pretty close. It is fast, wind doesn't seem to trouble it much, and it uses less fuel than other types. It has a built-in starter to get things going, and everything fits nicely in the metal canister for packing.

COOKWARE AND EATING UTENSILS

For more than a decade I packed an aluminum cooking kit that I purchased in 1961, when my wife and I began tent camping. It consisted of two frying pans (the cooking kit cover served as one), six plates, six cups, a one-quart pail with cover, a two-quart pail with cover, a coffee pot, and handles for the frying pans, all nestled together in a big aluminum pail that we used for washing dishes. We used one of the frying pans to rinse our washed dishes; the other served as a personal washbasin. Although the cooking kit was heavy and a bit dented, nothing leaked, nothing was broken, and it served us well. It was built to last.

In 1996 we left behind the aluminum cooking kit. I stored it on my camping storage shelf in the basement, where it stands today, with many stories to tell. The replacement is a set of titanium cook pots that nestle together and weigh little. We no longer bring along plates, and we pack only two regular-size plastic coffee cups, which we use for soup. For coffee, Steve and I each have an insulated coffee cup with a cover to keep the coffee warm for long periods. Our eating utensils include hard plastic spoons and forks. We each have a Swiss Army knife with small and large blades (and a bottle and can opener, toothpick, tweezers, and an awl). For a backup I also have my Leatherman, which I keep fastened to my belt at all times. (Looks good as well as being functional.)

I know what I'm about to share probably doesn't fit the approach many would take while camping, but we eat all of our meals out of plastic bowls. Our dish washing is minimal, the weight of our equipment is nil. Of course, our cooking equipment precludes serving certain kinds of meals. We've given up on pancakes—too many problems with sticky syrup bottles and sticky plates to wash. Nothing baked. Nothing fried. Nothing fancy.

In summary, our cook kit since 2003 consists of three cups, two bowls, three spoons, one titanium cook kit—considerably less than when we began canoe camping in 1983.

CANTEENS

I have two old-fashioned, two-quart, western-style fabric-covered canteens. Each has a canvas strap long enough to fit over my shoulder. To keep the contents cool on a hot summer day while in camp, you simply wet the fabric cover and the evaporation cools the water inside.

DISHWASHING NEEDS

Camp rule: Whoever owns the camp stove does the cooking, and the cook does not do dishes. For many years I cooked, and Steve washed dishes. Since Steve bought his new quick-heating Jetboil stove, he has been camp cook, and I've become the cleanup guy.

Our dishwashing equipment includes a small plastic container of biodegradable dish soap, a small scraper, and a dish towel. Since our cooking utensils have shrunk to bowls, cups, and spoons, we wash dishes in one of the cooking pots and rinse them in another. One thing I learned from way back in my army days is to rinse everything with boiling water. Nothing can result in more unhappiness in camp than an upset stomach caused by soap residue on dishes. Always toss used dishwater a good distance from the lake.

A big roll of paper towels is indispensable. We use heavy-duty paper towels for napkins, for cleaning up spills, and yes, a sheet or two can surely help start a difficult campfire. We've learned the hard way to keep it dry. One year I forgot to put the towels under cover during a hard rain and the roll of towels did what it's designed to do: soak up water. No more paper towels that year.

With the dishwashing equipment, I pack a clothesline—a light rope, about 15 feet long—and a dozen or so old-fashioned wooden clothespins. I string the clothesline between a couple trees, away from where we ordinarily walk, and dry everything there, from dish towels to wet bathing suits.

KITCHEN FLY

For our second year camping in the BWCAW, I purchased a 10 x 12-foot ripstop nylon fly to hang over the cooking area during wet weather. We tie a rope to each corner and tie the other ends to an appropriate tree, sometimes spending more time than we should discussing such profound questions as, "Which trees will give us just the right slant on the cooking fly, so as to shed water, keep us dry, but not block a view of the lake." It seems the priority of keeping dry is about on a par with a lake view—thus the need for the sometimes extended discussion.

WATER TREATMENT

No matter how clear and clean lake or river water appears, be aware that it might not be safe for drinking. A microscopic critter called *Giardia lamblia* or other contaminants may lurk in the water, unbeknownst to the camper. Giardia causes diarrhea and thus considerable discomfort and inconvenience, and even the potential for a completely ruined camping trip.

Some years ago, we began boiling all of our drinking and cooking water. We dip a cooking pot into the lake, searching for the clearest, cleanest water we can find, and then we boil it (with a rolling boil) for at least three minutes. Those who know more about water treatment than we suggest this is the best way to make sure water is safe.

Various water filters are also available, purporting to sift the beasties from the water. I've never used one so can't comment. For emergencies—if for some reason we can't boil water—I have along

Potable Aqua germicidal tablets, which are supposed to knock out *Giardia lamblia*. I haven't used these tablets for several years, but I remember that following the directions when using them was critical.

If you want fresh-caught fish for dinner, you have to filet them, which means removing the skin and bones before frying.

MENUS

I write our menus in my camping journal. They guide us in food purchasing and food preparation. Here is a typical menu (with grocery list) for five days of camping for two people:

BREAKFAST
- Instant oatmeal, assorted flavors (8 packages)
- Raisins (8 small boxes)

252

- Breakfast bars, assorted flavors (16)
- Coffee, instant Folger's in individual bags (50 bags—we drink coffee in midmorning, after lunch, midafternoon, and sometimes in the evening)

LUNCH
- Mixed nuts (1 plastic canister)
- Beef jerky (3 small bags that weigh about 3 to 6 ounces each)
- Bagels, plain, non-refrigerated type (18). Bagels travel well, keep well, and for us, replace bread and crackers. We eat them for lunch and for supper. Check the expiration date. One year I didn't, and by midweek our bagels began to mold. Not good.
- Strawberry jam (1 plastic squeezable container)
- Peanut butter (1 small plastic container)
- String cheese (24 individually wrapped sticks). We also eat cheese for supper on occasion.
- Snickers (12 full-size bars). It's the only time of the year that I eat and enjoy candy. Lots of quick energy here.

SUPPER
- Cup-of-Soup, various flavors (8). We like chicken noodle, vegetable, split pea, and tomato.
- Dried main dishes. These dried foods come in sealed pouches that travel well and will not spoil. Preparation directions are on the package.
- Cheddar Broccoli for two, dried (1)
- Beef Stroganoff and Noodles for two, dried (1)
- Mashed potato flakes (1)
- Spanish rice (1)
- Beef sausage log, non-refrigerated typed (1)

- Chocolate pudding (12 individual containers)
- Pepper and salt, in small individual containers
- Margarine (1 squeezable container)

Packed up and ready for the return trip home. Fingers of mist rise from the lake as we prepare to paddle out.

Since our first couple of camping trips, we have purchased all of our food at a grocery store near home. Larger grocery stores have a considerable selection of dried foods at a price that is considerably less than the cost of food especially prepared (and marketed) for campers.

We pack our food in zip-top bags of various sizes so it takes up considerably less room than the original packages. Be sure to cut preparation directions off boxes and include with the food in plastic bags.

Before we leave home, we sort the food and place it in three waterproof bags marked Breakfast, Lunch, and Supper. These we put in our big Duluth food Pack. By separating the food by meal, the cook doesn't have to dig through a food pack looking for something for supper that is under the breakfast stuff.

We bring along several large, heavyweight garbage bags. All trash goes in one. Remember, everything brought into the BWCAW must be taken out, especially all trash.

Several years ago we switched from catching and eating fish to catching and releasing it. It was a tough decision, because fresh-caught fish makes a tasty camp meal. But now we leave the heavy skillet at home, and another fairly messy cleanup has joined our camp cooking history.

We eat simple foods, simply prepared but heartily enjoyed, for our appetites flourish while canoe camping.

Bibliography

BOOKS

Apps, Jerry. *Blue Shadows Farm*. Madison: Univ. of Wisconsin Press, 2009.

———. *Cabin in the Country*. Wautoma, WI: Argus Publishing, 1973.

———. *Cranberry Red*. Madison: Univ. of Wisconsin Press, 2010.

———. *The Land Still Lives*. Madison: Wisconsin House, 1970.

———. *Old Farm: A History*. Madison: Wisconsin Historical Society Press, 2008.

Beymer, Robert. *Boundary Waters Canoe Area: The Eastern Region*. Berkeley, CA: Wilderness Press, 2000.

———. *Boundary Waters Canoe Area: The Western Region*. Berkeley, CA: Wilderness Press, 2009.

Carson, Rachel. *Silent Spring*. Boston: Houghton Mifflin, 1962.

Christofferson, Bill. *The Man from Clear Lake: Earth Day Founder Senator Gaylord Nelson*. Madison: Univ. of Wisconsin Press, 2004.

Dunning, Joan. *The Loon: Voice of the Wilderness*. Boston: Houghton Mifflin, 1985.

Emerson, Ralph Waldo. *Nature and Other Writings*. Boston: Shambhala, 2003 (first published 1854).

Jacobson, Cliff. *Boundary Waters Canoe-camping, 2nd Ed.* Guilford, CT: Globe Pequot, 2000.

Heinselman, Miron. *The Boundary Waters Wilderness Ecosystem*. Minneapolis: Univ. of Minnesota Press, 1996.

Kephart, Horace. *Camping and Woodcraft*. New York: Macmillan, 1917.

Klein, Tom. *Loon Magic*. Ashland, WI: Paper Birch Press, 1985.

Leopold, Aldo. *A Sand County Almanac*. New York: Oxford Univ. Press, 1949.

Louv, Richard. *Last Child in the Woods*. Chapel Hill, NC: Algonquin Books, 2006.

Muir, John. *The Story of My Boyhood and Youth*. New York: Houghton Mifflin, 1913.

Nute, Grace Lee. *The Voyageur*. Minneapolis: Univ. of Minnesota Press, 1931, 1955, 1987.

Olson, Sigurd. *Listening Point*. Minneapolis: Univ. of Minnesota Press, 1958, 1997.

———. *The Singing Wilderness*. Minneapolis: Univ. of Minnesota Press, 1956, 1997.

Pauly, Daniel. *Exploring the Boundary Waters*. Minneapolis: Univ. of Minnesota Press, 2005.

Proescholdt, Kevin, Rip Rapson, and Miron L. Heinselman. *Troubled Waters: The Fight for the Boundary Waters Canoe Area Wilderness*. St. Cloud, MN: North Star Press, 1995.

Rutstrum, Calvin. *Once Upon a Wilderness*. Minneapolis: Univ. of Minnesota Press, 1973, 2002.

———. *The Wilderness Life*. Minneapolis: Univ. of Minnesota Press, 1975, 2004.

Scott, Doug. *Our Wilderness: America's Common Ground*. Golden, CO: Fulcrum Publishing, 2009.

Sivertson, Howard. *The Illustrated Voyageur*. Duluth, MN: Lake Superior Port Cities, 1994.

Thoreau, Henry David. *Walden*. New York: W.W. Norton, 1951 (first published 1854).

OTHER PUBLICATIONS

Boundary Waters Journal, Ely, MN

Canoe and Kayak magazine, San Clemente, CA

Duluth News Tribune, Duluth, MN

Star Tribune, Minneapolis-St. Paul, MN

WEBSITES
www.jerryapps.com
www.steveapps.com

GRAND MARAIS, MN
Grand Marais Area Tourism Association, www.grandmarais
.com (history, businesses, outfitters)

LAKE SUPERIOR
Great Lakes Information Network, www.great-lakes.net/lakes/
ref/supfact.html (history, lore, statistics)

HISTORY OF THE BOUNDARY WATERS CANOE AREA WILDERNESS
Backes, David. "The Life of Sigurd F. Olson." www4.uwm.edu/
letsci/research/sigurd_olson.
Superior National Forest. "History of the Boundary Waters
Canoe Area Wilderness." www.fs.fed.us/r9/forests/superior/
bwcaw/bwhist.php.
Superior National Forest. "Special Places: Boundary Waters
Canoe Area Wilderness." www.fs.usda.gov/wps/portal/
fsinternet/!ut/p/c5/04.
Wilbers, Stephen. "Boundary Waters Chronology." www
.wilbers.com/BoundaryWatersCanoeAreaWilderness
ChronologyWelcome.htm.

CAMPING IN BEAR COUNTRY
American Bear Association, www.americanbear.org/contact
.html.
Center for Wildlife Information. "Be Bear Aware." www
.bebearaware.com.
Rogers, Lynn L. "Camping with Bears." www.bwca.cc/
wildlife/bears/campingwithbears.htm.

CANOE HISTORY
Hudson's Bay Company. "Our History: Transportation and
Technology." www.hbc.com/hbcheritage/history/transpor
tation/canoe/default.asp?pm=1.
White Oak Society, Inc. "Canoes." www.whiteoak.org/learning/
canoes.htm.

Notes

INTRODUCTION

1. Henry David Thoreau, *Walden* (New York: W. W. Norton, 1854, 1951), 28.
2. Richard Louv, *Last Child in the Woods* (Chapel Hill, NC: Algonquin Books, 2006), 7.

2—FOUNDATIONS

1. Ralph Waldo Emerson, *Nature and Other Writings* (Boston and London: Shambhala, 1836, 2003), 5.
2. Aldo Leopold, *A Sand County Almanac* (New York: Oxford Univ. Press, 1949), 200.
3. Sigurd Olson, *The Singing Wilderness* (Minneapolis: Univ. of Minnesota Press, 1958, 1997), 5.
4. Gaylord Nelson, "Speech Notes" (Madison: Wisconsin Historical Society Digital Collection, Madison Earth Day Speech Notes, 1970), 2.
5. Calvin, Rutstrum, *The Wilderness Life* (Minneapolis: Univ. of Minnesota Press, 1975, 2004), 211–212.
6. Ibid., 215.

5—GRAND MARAIS

1. Terry Pepper, "Grand Marais Light," www.terrypepper .com/lights/superior/gdmarais-mn/index.htm; Grand Marais Area Tourism Association, "Marina/Harbor," http://grandmarais.com/lake/lake.php?page=Marina%20 and%20Harbor.

6—A Brief History of the BWCAW

1. Superior National Forest, "History of the Boundary Waters Canoe Area Wilderness," www.fs.fed.us/r9/forests/superior/bwcaw/bwhist.php.
2. Superior National Forest, "Special Places: Boundary Waters Canoe Area Wilderness," www.fs.usda.gov/wps/portal/fsinternet/!ut/p/c5/04.
3. Stephen Wilbers, "Boundary Waters Chronology," www.wilbers.com/BoundaryWatersCanoeAreaWilderness ChronologyWelcome.htm, 1–3.
4. Ibid., 2–5.
5. Grace Nee Nute, *The Voyageur* (Minneapolis: Minnesota Historical Society Press, 1931, 1955), 13–14.
6. Ibid., 24.
7. Howard Sivertson, *The Illustrated Voyageur* (Duluth, MN: Lake Superior Port Cities, 1999), 11.
8. Nute, *Voyageur*, 64.
9. Sivertson, *Illustrated Voyageur*, 36–40.
10. Wilbers, "Boundary Waters Chronology," 7.
11. Kevin Proescholdt, Rip Rapson, and Miron L. Heinselman, *Troubled Waters: The Fight for the Boundary Waters Canoe Area Wilderness* (St. Cloud, MN: North Star Press, 1995), xii–xiv.
12. Wilbers, "Boundary Waters Chronology," 11.
13. Proescholdt et al., *Troubled Waters*, xiii.
14. Wilbers, "Boundary Waters Chronology," 9.
15. Superior National Forest, "History of the Boundary Waters Canoe Area Wilderness," www.fs.fed.us/r9/forests/superior/bwcaw/bwhist.php.
16. Wilbers, "Boundary Waters Chronology," 6.
17. Ibid., 10.
18. Ibid., 11.
19. Proescholdt et al., *Troubled Waters*, xiv–xvi.
20. Wilbers, "Boundary Waters Chronology," 13.
21. Ibid., 17.
22. Wilderness Act, Public Law 88-577 (16 U.S. C. 1131-1136), 1964.
23. Proescholdt et al, *Troubled Waters*, xiv–xvi.
24. Boundary Waters Canoe Area Wilderness Act of 1978, Public Law 95-495.

9—BEARS

1. Lynn L. Rogers, "Camping with Bears," www.bwca.cc/ wildlife/bears/campingwithbears.htm.

10—LOONS AND OTHER WILDLIFE

1. Sigurd T. Olson, preface to *Loon Magic*, ed. Tom Klein (Ashland, WI: Paper Birch Press, 1985), vii.
2. Tom Klein, *Loon Magic* (Ashland, WI: Paper Birch Press, 1985), vii.
3. Minnesota Department of Natural Resources, "Common Loon," www.dnr.state.mn.us/snapshots/birds/common-loon.html.

18—ROUGH WATER

1. Mayo Clinic, "Hypothermia," www.mayoclinic.com/ health/hypothermia/DS00333.
2. Ibid.

19—WIND AND FIRE

1. Peter S. Parke and Norvan J. Larson, "July 4–5, 1999 Derecho, 'The Boundary Waters-Canadian Derecho,'" www.spc .noaa.gov/misc/AbtDerechos/casepages/jul4-51999page.htm.
2. Stephen Wilbers, "Boundary Waters Chronology," www .wilbers.com/BoundaryWatersCanoeAreaWilderness ChronologyWelcome.htm.
3. Ada Igoe, "Wind, Fire and Growth," *Boundary Waters Journal*, Fall 2009, 68–74.
4. "The Cavity Lake Fire in the Boundary Waters Canoe Area Is Almost Over," *Minneapolis-St. Paul Star Tribune*, August 8, 2006.
5. Elizabeth Stawicki and Steve Karnowski, "Man Charged with Causing 2007 Ham Lake Forest Fire," Minnesota Public Radio/Associated Press, October 21, 2008.
6. Bob Kelleher, Minnesota Public Radio, May 20, 2008.
7. Larry Oakes, "Stephen Posniak: 'Casualty of Ham Lake Fire,'" *Minneapolis-St. Paul Star Tribune*, December 18, 2008.

20—THE STATE BIRD OF MINNESOTA

1. Horace Kephart, *Camping and Woodcraft* (New York: Macmillan, 1917), 244.

21—CANOES

1. "The History of the Canoe," www.canoe.ca/AllAboutCanoes.

22—TENTS

1. Horace Kephart, *Camping and Woodcraft* (New York: Macmillan, 1917), 68.

23—EQUIPMENT AND CLOTHING

1. Horace Kephart, *Camping and Woodcraft* (New York: Macmillan, 1917), 25–26.
2. Ibid., 138.